UNDERSTANDING THE GENERAL INSTRUCTION OF THE ROMAN MISSAL

GERARD MOORE

Paulist Press
New York/Mahwah, NJ

Having received the favorable recommendation of Rev. John Frauenfelder, STD, regarding the theological analysis of the *General Instruction of the Roman Missal* by Gerard Moore, BA, BTh, STL, STD, I hereby grant the Imprimatur in accordance with C. 830 § 3. Given at the Chancery Office in Broken Bay this twenty-ninth day of November, 2005.

+ The Most Reverend David L. Walker, DD, MTh
Bishop of Broken Bay

Reverend Colin Munday,
Vicar General

Scripture extracts are taken from the New Revised Standard Version, Copyright © 1989, by the Division of Christian Education of the National Council of the Churches of Christ in the United States of America and reprinted by permission of the publisher.

Extracts from the documents of the Second Vatican Council are the author's translation and from Walter Abbot's edition of *The Documents of Vatican II* © 1966 by America Press used by kind permission of America Press. Visit: www.americamagazine.org.

The English translation of the Directory for Masses with Children from *Documents on the Liturgy, 1963–1979: Conciliar, Papal, and Curial Text,* © 1982, International Committee on English in the Liturgy, Inc. (ICEL); excerpts from the English translation of *The General Instruction of the Roman Missal,* © 2002, ICEL. All rights reserved.

Cover and book design by Lynn Else

Copyright © 2007 by Gerard Moore

Library of Congress Cataloging-in-Publication Data

Moore, Gerard.
    Understanding the general instruction of the Roman missal / Gerard Moore.
        p.   cm.
    Includes bibliographical references.
    ISBN 978-0-8091-4452-5 (alk. paper)
    1. Missals. 2. Catholic Church—Liturgy—Texts. I. Title.
BX2015.M66 2007
264'.02036—dc22

                                                                2006035341

Published by Paulist Press
997 Macarthur Boulevard
Mahwah, New Jersey 07430
www.paulistpress.com

Printed and bound in the United States of America

CONTENTS

Contents

CONTENTS

To Bishop Maurice Taylor and Dr. John Page
in appreciation

ACKNOWLEDGMENTS

My thanks to Neil Brown who set in place at the Catholic Institute of Sydney the book-leave provisions under which this publication was able to come to light and to the faculty of the Institute for their encouragement. I would like to acknowledge the efforts of Tom Elich, Russell Hardiman, and Peter Williams who generously read various parts of the manuscript and offered many stimulating views and critiques of the work as it progressed. Finally I would like to close with an appreciation of the willing and careful help of Peter Finn at ICEL, who sorted through the various versions and translations of the *Instruction* itself.

ABBREVIATIONS

DMC   The Directory for Masses with Children
DV   The Dogmatic Constitution on Divine Revelation,
          Dei verbum
GIRM The *General Instruction of the Roman Missal*
SC   The Constitution on the Sacred Liturgy,
          Sacrosanctum concilium

INTRODUCTION

The purpose of this Instruction is to offer general guidelines for arranging the eucharistic celebration properly and to set forth the rules of ordering the individual forms of celebration. (21)

What sort of guide is the *General Instruction of the Roman Missal* (herein GIRM)? It sits neatly at the front of the Roman Missal, often unread and little understood. Yet it is offered to us as a guidebook and set of working rules for our celebration. What then does it say? More importantly, what are the underlying principles and theologies that give shape to its contents? This book is an attempt to explore the inner dynamics and theological streams at the heart of the *Instruction*. The more we understand these, the more we are able to take the GIRM as our guide, interpret it accurately, and apply it to our every celebration. The 2002 publication of a new edition of the *Institutio* provides us with an opportunity to look at it with fresh eyes, especially in light of our almost forty years' experience of the renewed liturgy.

There have been surprisingly few studies of the *Instruction*. A number of books have addressed the practical implementation of its guidelines and rules. That is not our task, however. Rather, this book is an attempt to read the work as closely as possible for the theological dynamics that lie underneath. In this it is part explanation and part commentary. As explanation, we will be seeking a theological appreciation of the content of the GIRM. As commentary, we will cast a critical eye over the document, highlighting strengths, weaknesses, inconsistencies, developments, and tensions. This will also involve teasing out the implications of the scriptural passages and patristic citations used to support various liturgical positions and assertions.

We open with an examination of the principles of interpretation that are found throughout the GIRM and that inform its theology and practice. Chapter 2 looks at some explicitly theological themes that can be found across the *Instruction:* How the document understands "tradition"; the relationship of the Mass from Vatican II to that from the Council of Trent; the contribution the GIRM makes to the discussion of unity; the adequacy of its theology of symbol; and the sense it accords the liturgical term *lex orandi lex credendi*? Chapter 3 contains a review of the theology of church in the *Instruction,* a central concern since the GIRM is insistent that the mystery of the church is revealed in the eucharistic celebration. Consequently it is worth exploring how the *Instruction* understands who we are and who we become as we engage in this sacred action. This is taken a step further in chapter 4, which examines the people of God understood hierarchically. There are important questions here, not the least of which involves the liturgical sense of the hierarchical church and what this may have to offer discussions of the meaning of hierarchy. We close our study with a chapter dedicated to the way the GIRM portrays the eucharistic celebration itself, with particular reference to its trinitarian underpinnings. In effect, our study concentrates on the theological currents that make up the *Instruction.* The clearer we are about them, the richer our understanding of the *Institutio,* and the more prayerful and powerful our liturgical practice.

The hope is that the book is accessible to bishops, priests, deacons, pastoral associates, members of diocesan, parish, and school liturgy teams, seminarians, and all with an interest in liturgy. In doing this I have tried to stay as close as possible to the 2002 edition of the GIRM itself. It is frequently quoted, both to give credibility to the interpretations offered, and as a method of making us all more familiar with the text itself. There are very few footnotes; they have been added only when I felt there was a need for further reference material or the sources were more difficult to find. As well, I have avoided making too many comparisons between different editions of the *Instruction*. Such things are of interest to scholars but do not make much of a difference to our practice and interpretation.

The translation followed is that of the International Commission on English in the Liturgy (ICEL) as adapted and published by the United States Conference of Catholic Bishops (USCCB). Each Conference of Bishops across the English-speaking world will produce a slightly modified version of this text. The USCCB edition follows the Latin original with a closeness that is often stultifying, unfortunately leaving the text a little too hard to read in places. Scriptural quotations are taken from the New Revised Standard Version (NRSV). Excerpts from the Second Vatican Council have been taken from Walter M. Abbott, general editor, *The Documents of Vatican II* (London: Geoffrey Chapman, 1967).

Throughout the book our document is variously referred to by its acronym, GIRM, the first word in its English name, *Instruction,* and the first word in its Latin title, *Institutio.* All are used interchangeably.

The General Instruction of the Roman Missal is one of the most underrated documents of the renewal of the liturgy and the church. It is a guide to the reform of the Mass and its proper celebration. It offers a broad and rich understanding of the Eucharist, challenging many of our presuppositions and practices. It is not without its tensions, which I hope are also brought out in the pages that follow. Nor is it beyond critique. My hope is that the better we know these riches, treasures, tensions, and limitations, the more we will become a truly eucharistic church and a foretaste of the reign of God.

CHAPTER ONE

PRINCIPLES OF INTERPRETATION

Finally, in this manner the liturgical norms of the Council of Trent have certainly been completed and perfected in many respects by those of the Second Vatican Council, which has brought to realization the efforts of the last four hundred years to bring the faithful closer to the sacred Liturgy especially in recent times, and above all the zeal for the Liturgy promoted by Saint Pius X and his successors. (15)

We begin our study with an examination of the *General Instruction of the Roman Missal* for the key principles it offers for interpreting the liturgy and applying the options the Missal offers. There is no single section detailing the principles. Rather the five points of interpretation that are developed here are drawn from a close reading of the text. They are an attempt to reflect on the grounds upon which the *Instruction* is built. While there may be others hidden among the many layers of thought and praxis in the *Institutio,* these five appear to be the mainstay of the work. They allow us to see the inner logic of the text as a whole and provide us with a set of interpretative keys to unlock rubrics, make choices, and appraise the strengths and weaknesses of the document.

Accordingly, the GIRM can be seen to offer worshippers five key principles for interpreting our celebration of the Mass. The first two are that our celebration of the

Eucharist should be pastorally effective and, as such, should encourage full, active, and conscious participation by all. The third is that to achieve these, we need to be attentive to the genres and functions of each rite, prayer, building, furnishing—in short whatever we do or use. The fourth is that our actions and objects ought to reflect appropriate standards of dignity, beauty, and solemnity. Finally, in light of all this, the *Instruction* desires that our celebration go beyond mere attention to the rubrics, and reflect the very spirit of the Sacred Liturgy itself.

THE PASTORAL PRINCIPLE

The chapter in the GIRM dealing with the choice of the Mass and its parts opens with a refreshing text:

> *The pastoral effectiveness of a celebration will be greatly increased if the texts of the readings, the prayers, and the liturgical songs correspond as closely as possible to the needs, spiritual prepa-ration, and culture of those taking part. This is achieved by appropriate use of the wide options described below.* (352)

The text embodies one of the key principles for under-standing the *General Instruction* and interpreting its provi-sions: the "pastoral effectiveness" of each celebration of the Eucharist.

Before this principle is applied to our current liturgy, the *General Instruction* acknowledges that it has been at work throughout the history of the church. The *Instruction* sees that the question on the use of the vernacular in the liturgy as discussed at the Council of Trent was resolved in light of the conditions of the age, a judgment of a pastoral nature (11). The Second Vatican Council is said to reflect the same pastoral concern in its deliberations on the issue: *Therefore, when the Second Vatican Council convened in* order to accommodate the Church to the requirements of her proper apostolic office precisely in these times, it examined thoroughly, as had Trent, the instructive and pastoral character of the sacred Liturgy (12). In fact, the Instruction writes that the council fathers were responding in ways unforeseen in the sixteenth century, and that they recognized that a different time in world history required different proposals and measures of a pastoral nature (10, 23). There is a clear expression of this underlying pastoral principle in the section on Communion under both kinds, with a reminder that this should be taught to the faithful:

> They are also to teach, furthermore, that the Church, in her stewardship of the Sacraments, has the power to set forth or alter whatever provisions, apart from the substance of the Sacraments, that she judges to be most conducive to the veneration of the Sacraments and the well-being of the recipients, in view of the changing conditions, times, and places. (282)

Finally, the Instruction contains the reminder that pastoral effectiveness involves the possibility of further revision and change: Finally, if the participation of the faithful and their spiritual welfare require variations and more thorough-going adaptations in order that the sacred celebration respond to the culture and conditions of the different peoples, then the Bishops' Conference may propose such... (395).

How, then, does the Instruction apply this broad theological and liturgical principle to the actual liturgy? While there is overlap between them, the GIRM speaks of three categories: the needs of the participants, their spiritual well-being and preparation, and their capacity (352). We will take up each in turn. The Institutio also relates pastoral effectiveness to active participation; however, we will examine participation in its own right below.

When discussing the homily, the Instruction urges the homilist to be attentive to the mystery being celebrated or

3

the needs proper to the listener (65). Many expressions and prayers of the Missal were adapted in light of the needs and circumstances of the contemporary world (15). The very existence in the Missal of Masses and prayers for various circumstances is a response to felt needs: ...*the Missal provides formularies for Masses and orations that may be used in the various circumstances of Christian life, for the needs of the whole world, or for the needs of the Church, whether universal or local* (368). Broad permission is given for their use when serious need or pastoral advantage call for it, even overriding important feasts and seasons in the calendar (374, 376). Pastoral considerations are paramount in the planning and choosing of the variable parts for a Mass for the Dead, especially the funeral Mass (385).

On a number of occasions the *Instruction* is attentive to the spiritual well-being of the assembly. It is to be at the fore when making choices and arranging the celebration:

> ...*the utmost care must be taken to choose and to arrange those forms and elements set forth by the Church that, in view of the circumstances of the people and the place, will more effectively foster active and full participation and more properly respond to the spiritual needs of the faithful.* (20)

This is applied directly to choices about movement and posture, where the spiritual good of the people is to be valued above private inclination or arbitrary choice (42). There is a call for appropriate periods of silence between the readings to allow for the workings of the Spirit, with the recommendation that the pauses be accommodated to the actual assembly gathered (56). The decision to move away from the restrictions from Trent and to allow the laity to share more fully in the Blood of Christ at Communion is related to the well-being of the recipients (282). Devotional practices and objects, including images, should be congruent with the entire community (318, 375) and not imposed (357).

4

The capacity of the gathered assembly features repeatedly in the *Instruction*. Any planning that is serious about the active participation of the faithful needs to take into account the nature and circumstances of each liturgical assembly (18). This includes the singing: *Great importance should therefore be attached to the use of singing in the celebration of the Mass, with due consideration for the culture of the people and abilities of each liturgical assembly* (40). Here we can see that cultural considerations are central in any discussion of what an assembly may or may not be capable of achieving. Similarly, cultural considerations play a part in choices around the rite of peace (82). The choice of readings, when that is an option, is to be guided by pastoral reasons (359, 361), such as the capacity of the people to hear and understand a long text (360). The posture of the people during the Mass is also regulated by their capacity to take up what is required. We can see this with regard to kneeling during the Eucharistic Prayer as set out for the dioceses of the United States: ...*they should kneel...except when prevented on occasion by reasons of health, lack of space, the large number of people present, or some other good reason* (43).

The importance the *Instruction* gives to pastoral considerations reflects the pastoral imperative within the celebrating community itself. The directives for the content of the general intercessions call the community to a pastoral sense of the condition of the church, the world at large, and their own local community (69). The poor are not to be forgotten at the preparation of the gifts (73). The rite of peace is said to exhibit something of the same character: *The Rite of Peace follows, by which the Church asks for peace and unity for herself and for the whole human family...* (82). The dismissal of the people at the conclusion of the Mass is related to doing good works (90). The Masses for Various Circumstances are not provided only for the needs of the praying assembly, but can reflect the assembly's care for the world and the church (368) in particular circumstances and occasions (369).

The *Instruction* is mindful of the place of the bishop and priest in the application and teaching of the principle itself. Pastoral effectiveness in the celebration is closely related to the role of the priest, who, as presiding celebrant, is to be aware of the nature and needs of the people in the assembly. Consequently, choices are to reflect the common spiritual good of the people rather than his own inclinations (352). Two examples provided are when there are special readings for a saint (357) and when there is an option to utilize a votive Mass (375). When dealing with questions of choice and pastoral care, the *Instruction* sometimes uses the term *pastor* for priest (282, 385). As well, clergy and people alike are to be taught the application of pastoral norms (396, 282).

THE PRINCIPLE OF PARTICIPATION

The principle of participation, in various forms, has been part of the process of liturgical reform that started in the late nineteenth century. The term *active participation* entered official language in a 1903 document from Pius X concerning sacred music in which he spoke about the liturgy as the source of sanctity for the people: *[the] foremost and indispensable fount, which is the active participation in the holy mysteries and in the public and solemn prayer of the Church.*[1] The principle, applied in the main to allow the people to sing their parts in the Gregorian chant, was developed by Pius XI and Pius XII.[2]

According to the *General Instruction* participation is a requirement for the celebration of the Mass, a point taken directly from the Constitution on the Sacred Liturgy, *Sacrosanctum concilium* (SC): *In the restoration and promotion of the sacred liturgy, this full and active participation by all the people is the aim to be considered before all else; for it is the primary and indispensable source from which the faithful are to derive the true Christian spirit* (SC 14). It is worth repeating one of the most quoted passages in the GIRM:

6

This will best be accomplished, if, with due regard for the nature and particular circumstances of each liturgical assembly, the entire celebration be planned in such a way that it leads to a conscious, active, and full participation of the faithful both in body and in mind, a participation burning with faith, hope, and charity, of the sort which is desired by the Church and demanded by the very nature of the celebration, and to which the Christian people have a right and duty by reason of their Baptism. (18 and 386)

How does the *Instruction* express these features? Participation is intimately linked to the ongoing conversion into holiness of the people of God: *Though holy in its origin, this people nevertheless grows continually in holiness by its conscious, active, and fruitful participation in the mystery of the Eucharist* (5). A footnote sets this sentence in the context of paragraph 11 in the Constitution on the Sacred Liturgy, where participation is related to the "full effectiveness" of the liturgy. In a similar vein, while discussing posture, the *Instruction* links the participation of all in the Mass to beauty, simplicity, and authentic celebration:

The gestures and posture of the priest, the deacon, and the ministers, as well as those of the people, ought to contribute to making the entire celebration resplendent with beauty and noble simplicity, so that the true and full meaning of the different parts of the celebration is evident and that the participation of all is fostered. (42)

Fruitful participation in the word of God is understood to enable us to grasp the scriptures in our hearts and to make a response (56). The same can be seen in the *Instruction*'s description of the Eucharistic Prayer where our learning to offer ourselves is related to our ongoing perfection in God (79f.). On a number of occasions participation is explicitly linked with the reception of Holy Communion (5, 13, 14, 282). These paragraphs refer in particular to restrictions on the reception of the cup by the faithful stemming from the Council of Trent. At the same time they remind us that Trent also encouraged frequent Communion, a reform that was not taken up until centuries later. The most important point, however, is around conversion into the Body of Christ: *Finally, it is a people made one by sharing in the Communion of Christ's Body and Blood* (5).

The *Instruction* approaches participation within worship from two further angles: the forms of the prayers and the forms of ministry. The GIRM invites our participation according to the various forms of prayer in the liturgy. We will take this up more fully below in our discussion of genre, however, two examples here will make the point. The acclamations, responses, prayers of the entire assembly, and dialogues are considered integral to the liturgy (34–36). Participation in them constitutes our worship and brings about the unity of the assembly: *The acclamations and the responses of the faithful to the priest's greetings and prayers constitute that level of active participation that the gathered faithful are to contribute in every form of the Mass, so that the action of the entire community may be clearly expressed and fostered* (35). One of the most important forms of prayer is singing. The *Instruction* ties singing closely to participation, whether Gregorian chant or music of another type: *Other types of sacred music, in particular polyphony, are in no way excluded, provided that they correspond to the spirit of the liturgical action and that they foster the participation of all the faithful* (41). Participation is likewise stressed when the GIRM discusses the role of the choir among the faithful (103).

The liturgy depends on the members of the faithful taking up their appropriate roles in ministry: *For the celebration of the Eucharist is an action of the whole Church, and in it each one should carry out solely but completely that which pertains to him or her, in virtue of the rank of each within the People of God* (5). Different members of the church will participate differently, according to the hierarchical order to which they belong: *It [the eucharistic celebration] also affects the individual members of the Church in different ways, according to their different orders, offices and actual participation* (91). This aspect of participation can be negated if the presiding celebrant considers the liturgy "his," or the organist takes "custody" of the music. On another point, the insistence in the GIRM on the differentiation of roles and ministries, and consequently the different experiences of participation in the one assembly, warns against the consideration that participation is "doing something." Rather, it is prayerful activity in light of the forms of the prayer and the functions of the ministries. Active participation in worship should allow God to "do" things so that our further conversion can take place.

Participation is promoted and protected across the GIRM as a whole. The introduction of the vernacular to the Mass (12) and the provision of suitable readings (391) and translations (392) aims to heighten participation. The arrangement and furnishing of church buildings ought to foster active participation: *Churches, therefore, and other places should be suitable for carrying out the sacred action and for ensuring the active participation of the faithful* (288). The building should be planned to allow all the participants to take their proper place and carry out effectively their proper functions (294). Consequently, care is to be taken to ensure that the faithful can easily see the sacred action (295), that they can readily focus on the altar (299) and ambo (309), and that the choir members can fulfill their roles and also receive Communion (312). The *Institutio* reinforces the importance of the lines of sight when discussing the place of concelebrating priests during the Mass:

> ...the concelebrants approach the altar and stand around it, but in such a way that they do not obstruct the execution of the rites and that the sacred action may be seen clearly by the faithful. They should not

> *be in the deacon's way whenever he needs to go to the altar to perform his ministry.* (215)

This sentence is also attentive to the need for ministers to be able to carry out their respective functions unimpeded.

The church building itself should also be a constant reminder of our participation in the liturgy. Somewhat meekly, the GIRM expresses the desire that the participation of the faithful be brought out in an offering of bread and wine, or gifts for the church or poor during the preparation of the gifts (73, 140). We can use this to go a little further. The church itself, its furnishings, art, vessels, and vestments have all come from the faithful. This is a form of participation that can be too easily and sadly overlooked.

Alongside this, there is a further level of participation in the building. The *Instruction* mandates the bishop and all involved with construction to consult the diocesan commission charged with oversight of sacred art and architecture (291). The aim is to ensure that decisions about architecture and furnishings are not idiosyncratic or simply authoritarian, but themselves reflect the nature of the church and its authentic liturgical celebration. Hopefully the advice of the commission members would include a process of consultation with the faithful of the parish or community. The parishioners should, at the very least, have input into the discussion of their "contemporary needs" and appropriate standards of "comfort" (293).

The *Instruction* makes an important point about participation and devotions. In a section on sacred images it emphasizes that devotional objects should reflect the community, rather than individuals or separate groups: *Generally speaking, in the ornamentation and arrangement of a church as far as images are concerned, provision should be made for the devotion of the entire community as well as the beauty and dignity of the images* (318). Similarly, when it comes to choosing readings for a saint whose feast has no proper readings, the GIRM discourages selections for the benefit of individuals or small groups in the assembly. It encourages, as a norm, the use of the readings of the week (357). In both sections we see the *Instruction* discouraging devotions that are exclusive of the larger body of the assembly and that would inhibit the participation of many worshipers.

The closing chapter of the *Instruction* contains a paragraph that underlines the centrality of participation in our interpretation of the liturgy: *Finally, if the participation of the faithful and their spiritual welfare require variations and more thoroughgoing adaptations in order that the sacred celebration respond to the culture and traditions of the different peoples, then Bishops' Conferences may propose such to the Apostolic See...* (395). The Roman Mass, then, is not a finished work. Rather it seeks to be responsive to the actual participants so as to draw them further into the paschal mystery being celebrated.

GENRE AND FUNCTION

What do we think we are doing when we participate in a rite, gesture, or ministry? How can we celebrate the liturgy of the Eucharist if we are not clear about how to celebrate its parts? These questions involve our understanding the genre of a prayer or action and its function in the liturgy. The *General Instruction* is attentive to the role of genre and function in our worship and discusses them in relation to rites, texts, music, gesture, posture, ministries, architecture, furnishings, and vestments. In fact, it highlights the importance of this pair of principles in a comment about the role of the bishop as the guardian and promoter of the liturgy in his diocese: *The Bishop should therefore be determined that the priests, the deacons, and the lay Christian faithful grasp ever more deeply the genuine meaning of the rites and liturgical texts, and thereby be led to an active and fruitful celebration of the Eucharist* (22). As well, the sentence shows how closely the *Instruction* links knowledge of the genre and function to participation. Since my point here is only to illustrate the principle of genre and function, I will limit my remarks to the rites and the texts. That should be sufficient to sharpen our reading of the *Instruction*.

We begin, then, with the way that the *Instruction* elucidates the eucharistic liturgy itself. Above all, it calls for respect for the nature and genre of the Roman Missal in its entirety (389). The GIRM describes the Mass, as portrayed in the Missal, as comprising two main parts, the liturgy of the word and the liturgy of the Eucharist, with opening and concluding rites (28). It goes on to offer an interpretation of each of these four parts. The introductory rites aim to unite the assembly and prepare it to celebrate worthily. They are said to have the character of a beginning, an introduction, and a preparation (46). In the liturgy of the word the faithful are said to be nourished by the scriptures and respond with their petitions (55). The liturgy of the Eucharist is described in terms of the preparation of the gifts, the great prayer of thanksgiving, and Communion, all three based on Jesus' actions at the Last Supper (72). The description of the concluding rite is a model of brevity (90). What the *Instruction* has provided here is an instrument for preparing and evaluating our liturgical practice: Does our enactment of each of these rites correspond to their purpose?

In opening this question, the GIRM provides a more precise set of tools. Throughout the *Institutio* there are discussions on the nature of each of the individual ritual forms, prayers, and readings that make up the four sections of the Mass. We are offered among others an understanding of presidential prayers (30), dialogue prayers (34), the private prayers of the priest (33), acclamations (35), silence (45), and the Eucharistic Prayer (147). The GIRM recognizes that knowledge of the rites is an essential component in effective preparation of the celebration (111). It is also seen to be an integral component in the translation of readings and prayers (391, 392).

While it would be interesting to examine music, posture, gesture, and the other areas, the key question remains: Are we enacting each aspect of our worship in accord with its genre and function? There are, however, more issues to explore. One is the amount of flexibility that the *Instruction* has built into the genres and forms themselves. Looking at texts as an example, there are a variety of options in the responsorial psalm (61), the readings (356–62), and the Eucharistic Prayer (364–65). This same flexibility is found with regard to the ministries, furnishings, vestments, and the design of churches. It is not unlimited, as each option needs to be true to that part of the liturgy. Consequently, there are provisions limiting the types of chants that can be used in the order of the Mass (366). Similarly, there is a prohibition of non-biblical texts in place of the readings during the liturgy of the word (57). As well, there are directives concerning the ministers and the content of the prayers of the faithful aimed at preserving the integrity of the prayer (69–71).

Attention to genre and function also brings to the fore some of the tensions and complexities within the rite. The introductory rites seem far too complex in their appointed task of assembling and preparation. At times, the description that the *Instruction* offers of a particular prayer or rite indicates that its nature is unclear or poorly appropriated. We can see this in the discussion of the sacramental efficacy of the act of penitence (51) and the protestation that the rite of carrying the offerings has retained its power and spiritual significance despite the emasculation of the action (73). The analysis of the collect-style prayers is more suited to a particular theology of priesthood than to its original patristic interpretation, a point taken up in the discussion of the models of priesthood in chapter IV (54).

The principle of genre and function provides us with a critical tool for appraisal both of our performance of the liturgy and also of the integrity of the liturgy itself. It allows us to ask what is to happen when a particular liturgical genre is unsuited to a culture or idiom or language. The

Instruction is not closed to substantial adaptations in response to the culture and traditions of the faithful (395), and the principle of genre and function offers significant opportunity for review and revision.

DIGNITY, BEAUTY, AND SOLEMNITY

The celebration of the liturgy should be carried out with dignity, should be marked by beauty, and should be appropriately solemn. Our discussion of what the *Instruction* understands by these three features begins with acknowledging that they are not proposed as ends in themselves. Rather they are seen to serve the eucharistic action, the celebration of the mysteries: *Indeed, the character and beauty of the place and all its furnishings should foster devotion and show forth the holiness of the mysteries celebrated there* (294, also 288, 318). Also, the *Instruction* relates dignity and beauty to the principles of pastoral concern, participation, and attention to genre that are at the basis of the liturgy. We see this come through in the admonition to the bishop to lead his priests, deacons, and faithful to a deeper grasp of the rites, the texts, and active participation: *To the same end, he [the bishop] should also be vigilant that the dignity of these celebrations be enhanced. In promoting this dignity, the beauty of the sacred place, of music, and of art should contribute as greatly as possible* (22). The same point is made later in the GIRM when it discusses movement and posture, where beauty is related to clarity about the meaning of the parts and participation:

> *The gestures and postures of the priest, the deacon, and the ministers, as well as those of the people, ought to contribute to making the entire celebration resplendent with beauty and noble simplicity, so that the true and full meaning of the different parts*

*of the celebration is evident and that the participa-
tion of all is fostered.* (42)

The *Instruction* insists that each celebration of the
Eucharist be enacted with dignity and appropriate solemnity. It advises a period of silence before the liturgy begins
to enable the faithful to prepare themselves devoutly and
fittingly (45). Actions and processions are to be carried out
with a decorum in keeping with their genre (44). All are to
turn toward the ambo during the reading of the Gospel as
a mark of special reverence to the Gospel of Christ (133).
As well, there are occasions during the liturgy that call for
a profound bow as a sign of reverence and honor (275b).
The use of incense is optional in any form of the Mass, but
it is an expression of reverence and of prayer (276), and is
appropriate as the occasion suggests (49, 123).

On top of this, there are provisions for heightening the
solemnity of a liturgy. This is appropriate for Sundays,
solemnities, and major feasts. There are also other solemn
celebrations (68), but the GIRM does not specify what
these are nor does it provide any particular criteria for
them. Solemnity is enhanced by the inclusion of the creed
(68), the praying of the Sequence if one is provided (64), the
use of the prayers over the people or solemn blessings during the concluding rites (90b), the wearing of the dalmatic
by the deacon (118b), and the wearing of more precious
vestments even if not the color of the day (346g). The
solemnity of a particular occasion should have an effect on
the way the priest, deacon, and readers proclaim the various texts and prayers (38). On more solemn occasions, the
bishop may bless the people with the Book of the Gospels
(175). In all this it is worth noting that the GIRM does not
create or authorize the commonly seen category of
"solemn high Mass." Every Mass is to be celebrated with
appropriate dignity, and solemnity can be heightened if the
occasion calls for it. Solemnity is also not an excuse for
music and celebration that precludes participation and
obscures the nature of the prayers and rites.

Solemnity and dignity are not considered apart from either joy or beauty. Joy is mentioned rarely in the *Instruction*. It is placed, however, at the core of all singing in the celebration: *Singing is the sign of the heart's joy (cf Acts 2:46). Thus St. Augustine says rightly: 'Singing is for one who loves'* (39). This joyful activity ought to be part of our celebrations on Sundays and holy days of obligation, and even weekday Masses if possible (40).

The *Instruction* closely associates dignity and beauty. Beauty of place, music, and art (22) are especially related to the mysteries being celebrated: *Sacred buildings and requisites for divine worship should, moreover, be truly worthy and beautiful and be signs and symbols of heavenly realities* (288). The Book of the Gospels and the Lectionary are spoken about in the same way as the church building:

> In a special way, care must be taken that the liturgical books, particularly the 'Book of the Gospels' and the Lectionary, which are intended for the proclamation of the word of God and hence enjoy special veneration, really serve in a liturgical action as signs and symbols of heavenly realities and hence are truly worthy, dignified, and beautiful. (349)

It is worth recalling that the higher, heavenly realities are given to us by the living God through Christ in the Spirit. Our aesthetics must be firmly attached to the paschal mystery, not to the canons of art alone.

Beauty is applied to our liturgical buildings and books, as seen above, as well as to the vestments for all ministers (335) and images of saints (318). The sacred vessels are to be worthy, distinguished for liturgical use, and precious, all the while suited to their liturgical function (332). The *Instruction* is somewhat caught, however, when it comes to establishing criteria for what is beautiful. In response it places together two sets of ideas. The first is that the works ought to reflect the craft, precious materials, and artistic excellence of each region and people, as long as they nourish the faith of the community and correspond to the intended meaning and purpose. It is worth quoting the entire number:

> *Consequently, the Church constantly seeks the noble assistance of the arts and admits the artistic expressions of all peoples and regions. In fact, just as she is intent on preserving the works of art and the artistic treasures handed down from past centuries, and, insofar as necessary, on adapting them to new needs, so also she strives to promote new works of art that are in harmony with the character of each successive age.*
>
> *On account of this, in commissioning artists and choosing works of art to be admitted into a church, what should be required is that true excellence in art which nourishes faith and devotion and accords authentically with both the meaning and the purpose for which it is intended.* (289, 325)

We can see this option for local materials, craft, and design in the choices involved in the building of an altar (301), the manufacture of sacred vessels (332), and the design and fabric for vestments (342, 343).

The second idea is that the liturgy being celebrated is the Roman liturgy, which traditionally has exhibited a preference for nobility and simplicity in all things. Not only should works be suited to the culture and traditions of the community, but, according to the *Instruction,* they are to be characterized by restraint as well: *In this matter as well, a noble simplicity should be ensured such as is the best companion of genuine art* (325). The GIRM exhibits a preference for noble simplicity over ostentation (292), which extends to even the smallest detail: *Every effort should be made to ensure that even as regards objects of lesser importance the canons of art be appropriately taken into account and that noble simplicity come together with elegance* (351).

It is best to avoid here any extended debate on the accepted canons of art, though the liturgy has something to offer on that score. However, for us there is a need to understand two approaches, the artisans in their freedom and the Roman liturgy in its preference. Both need to be attentive to the theological imperative of the mysteries that we are celebrating, and, accordingly, seek buildings, vessels, vestments, and images that respect the community, enable participation, and are true to the genre of the rites, prayers, and actions.

THE SPIRIT OF THE CELEBRATION

There are a number of references in the *Instruction* to the spirit of the sacred liturgy. We have here an attempt to pull the liturgy away from being mere rubric and lifeless enactment, a point that comes from the Constitution on the Sacred Liturgy: *Pastors of souls must, therefore, realize that, when the liturgy is celebrated, their obligation goes further than simply ensuring that the laws governing valid and lawful celebration are observed* (SC 11). The Constitution also associates active participation in the liturgy with an ever-deepening appreciation of the true Christian spirit: *for [full, conscious, and active participation] is the primary and indispensable source from which the faithful are to derive the true Christian spirit* (SC 14).

The spirit of the liturgy first relates back to the very reason for our worship. Our eucharistic liturgy is an action of Christ and the church, his body, in celebration of the salvation that God continues to work for us through the paschal mystery and the gift of the Spirit. Our response, possible only in divine grace, is one of thanksgiving, communion, and ongoing conversion. Every celebration of the Mass should reflect this spirit, as should every Christian action.

The spirit of the liturgy is applied to the way in which we carry out the liturgy. The bishop is admonished that all the members of the church have a genuine sense of the rites and texts (22). On two occasions the GIRM puts together an appreciation of the norms for celebration with an understanding of the spirit of the liturgy. The first time we see this, both norms and spirit are put in the context of pastoral effectiveness, as are the adaptations and accommodations that the *Instruction* offers: *Moreover, in order that such a celebration may correspond more fully to the prescriptions and spirit of the sacred Liturgy, and also in order to increase its pastoral effectiveness, certain accommodations and adaptations are specified in this General Instruction and in the Order of the Mass* (23). Toward the close of the *Instruction* we have the same pairing of the norms and spirit, this time in relation to the full, active, and conscious participation of the people (386). We can see that, for the GIRM, the spirit of the liturgy comes to the fore when all the faithful—bishops, priests, deacons, and laity—have a genuine sense of the rites, understand the norms, participate fully, actively, and consciously, and take up all the options in light of the pastoral situation of the assembly.

This requires a certain liturgical spirituality. The *Institutio* reminds the presiding celebrant that his ministry requires more than turning up, dressing up, and speaking up: *When he celebrates the Eucharist, therefore, he must serve God and the people with dignity and humility, and by his bearing and by the way he says the divine words he must convey to the faithful the living presence of Christ* (93). The lay faithful, too, should evince a spirit marked by a deep religious sense and charity. They are to shun individualism and division, treat all present as their brothers and sisters, and form by their actions and attitudes one single body. They should also be willing to perform a particular function or ministry if asked (95–97).

The insistence on the spirit of the liturgy offers two vital challenges to our worship. First, it means we have to ask what sort of church we make manifest in our liturgy. Is it one whose only existence is in praise of salvation through the threefold God? The second challenge is that each act of worship is more than a ritualized performance, it is an experience of faith and conversion. If we do not experience the Mass as a celebration of praise and thanksgiving then our Eucharist cannot nourish our faith. This is worship without spirit, and it leaves us as worshipers increasingly distant from the Spirit.

CONCLUSION

The *Instruction* offers other minor interpretative tools. There are occasions where the GIRM praises some options as laudable (e.g., 43, 118, 122, 173). Local custom is given a role in the decision to ring bells at the showing of the host and chalice (150). However, the interpretative framework within the *Instruction* calls us to larger issues. Our worship needs to be pastorally effective, fully participatory, attentive to genre and function, and marked by beauty, dignity, and solemnity. It cannot be content with a mechanical reproduction of the rites. Rather, our way of celebrating and our choice of options should enable our liturgy to shine with the spirit of the Sacred Liturgy.

CHAPTER TWO

THEOLOGICAL THEMES

The Roman Rite constitutes a notable and precious part of the liturgical treasure and patrimony of the Catholic Church. Its riches are of benefit to the universal Church, so that were they to be lost, the Church would be seriously harmed. (397)

The *General Instruction* makes a contribution to an important set of theological questions. This is inevitable given that it aims to build upon the ever-increasing number of studies of the life and writings of the early church in all regions (8, 9), the controversies from the Reformation period (11), and the new requirements of the contemporary world (15). In particular five areas stand out. We begin by examining the contribution the *Instruction* makes to our understanding of tradition. This is complemented with a commentary on the relationship between the reform of Vatican II and that of the Council of Trent. Not unrelated to these two is the understanding in the *Instruction* of unity. Given that liturgy is ritual activity, it is important to discuss how the term *symbol* is used throughout the document. We will bring the chapter to a close with some observations on how the *Instruction* relates worship to doctrine, often referred to under the adage *lex orandi lex credendi*.

TRADITION

An important theological theme, central to the sense of the *Instruction,* is that of tradition. The word is used in a number of different ways, and it is described through a range of dynamics. What does it mean, then, to say that the GIRM presents us with a model of traditional worship?

To begin we will distinguish three uses of the word *tradition.* In the *Instruction* it appears to be applied to those liturgical things that belong to the core of the faith, to usages that reflect the ancient norms of the patristic era, and to practices that are customary.

The *Instruction* has set the Roman Rite within the broader apostolic tradition of authentic worship and doctrinal purity:

> *Furthermore, the principle shall be respected according to which each particular Church must be in accord with the universal Church not only regarding the doctrine of the faith and sacramental signs, but also as to the usages universally handed down by apostolic and unbroken tradition. These are to be maintained not only so that errors may be avoided, but also so that the faith may be passed on in its integrity, since the Church's rule of prayer* ("lex orandi") *corresponds to her rule of belief* ("lex credendi"). (397)

We can point to a number of aspects of the liturgy that fit the threefold criteria of being a doctrine of faith, a sacramental sign, and admitted by apostolic, unbroken tradition. The Mass itself, in particular the liturgy of the Eucharist within the Mass, is said to come from Christ and was handed on by him to the church to be carried out in his memory (72). This is seen constantly throughout the document, reflected, for example, in the use of bread and wine (319), and the provision of bread that can be easily broken and distributed to at least some of the faithful (321).

The *Instruction*'s insistence on the scriptural basis of the Mass falls into the same category. The readings are an essential aspect of the nourishment Christ offers and cannot be substituted with nonbiblical selections (57). Moreover, the scriptures are seen to be at the heart of every part of the liturgy:

> For it is out of the Sacred Scripture that the readings are read and explained in the homily and that psalms are sung, and it is drawing upon the inspiration and spirit Sacred Scripture that prayers, orations, and liturgical songs are fashioned in such a way that from them actions and signs derive their meaning. (391)

A third feature is the primacy of the Lord's Day: *In carrying this out, to the greatest extent possible the Lord's Day is to be preserved and safeguarded, as the primordial holy day, and hence other celebrations, unless they be truly of the greatest importance, should not have precedence over it* (394).

There are usages of the word *tradition* that reflect the practices of the first six or seven centuries in the life of the church, commonly known as the *patristic era*. The language of the *Instruction,* reflecting that in the 1570 Roman Missal, refers to the ancient "norm of the holy Fathers" (6). These norms are discovered from a number of sources, such as patristic scholarship in critical editions of liturgical texts and ongoing studies of the theology of the ancient writers (8). Yet the *Institutio* situates these within the larger framework of the faith as lived in each age, on the basis that this offers a window into the workings of the Spirit amid the church. The result is that the norms of the early centuries are not understood as timeless, unchangeable practices, but rather need to be reappropriated for each age:

> For this reason, the "norm of the holy Fathers" requires not only the preservation of what our immediate forebears have passed on to us, but also

> *an understanding and a more profound study of the Church's entire past and of all the ways in which her one and only faith has been set forth in the quite diverse human and social forms prevailing in the Semitic, Greek, and Latin areas. Moreover, this broader view allows us to see how the Holy Spirit endows the People of God with a marvellous fidelity in preserving the unalterable deposit of faith, even amid a very great variety of prayers and rites.* (9)

The GIRM explores the Council of Trent in this light, reflecting that Trent was concerned with the preservation of "more recent tradition" (7). The *Institutio* makes the same claim for the current Roman Missal, describing it as an authentic development of the liturgical tradition offering a new pastoral response in a different historical context (10).

There are a number of occasions where tradition as the norm of the patristic era is applied to rites and prayers. We see it in the description of the collect prayer (54), the ministerial rather than presidential nature of the proclamation of the readings (59), the use of a fixed stone altar (301), the deposition of a martyr's relics beneath an altar (302), the display and veneration of sacred images (318), and the choice of texts to be read at Easter (357). In general, the *Instruction* deals with those traditions most typical of the Roman Rite itself (42, 397). Here we can see the source of the preference for unleavened bread, wheaten and recently baked (320).

There are a number of practices that the *Instruction* labels as traditional, but which reflect more the level of long-standing custom. That does not mean they are held with less affection or defended with less vigor. We can include here the act of penitence rather than the asperges (51), the presence of a wax or oil lamp by the tabernacle (316), the traditional shape of the bread (321), the color of vestments (346), and the local diocesan calendar (355). The *Instruction* admits of some customs that are suited to a particular locality only, such as the ringing of the bell at the showing of the host and chalice in the Eucharistic Prayer (150) and some local customs concerning the position of the tabernacle in the church (314). When it comes to liturgical reform, there is an implicit reminder that long-standing practices and customs can inhibit the implementation of conciliar decrees, such as the determined resistance over centuries to the desire of the bishops at Trent that the faithful receive Holy Communion at each Mass (13).

Yet the discussion of tradition in the *Instruction* is not without an element of self-indulgence. The final chapter contains a rather extraordinary claim:

> *Throughout the ages, the Roman Rite has not only preserved the liturgical usages that arose in the city of Rome, but has also in a deep, organic, and harmonious way incorporated into itself certain other usages derived from the customs and culture of different peoples and of various particular Churches of both West and East, so that in this way, the Roman Rite has acquired a certain supraregional character.* (397)

History vouches for much of what is said here, especially regarding the various layers of texts in the rite that have been integrated from diverse peoples, cultures, and eras. However, whether this is organic and harmonious, or simply that we are accustomed to it, is another question. Moreover, we are dealing with a tradition that was formed first in the Roman Empire, both east and west, and then added to in western Europe. There are many Roman Catholics who are foreign to these cultures, and for whom the Roman Rite can appear to have many alien and arbitrary features. We need the wisdom to discern among the traditions that make our faith, those that are ancient, and those that are more customary; and we need the understanding to reappropriate them in light of different cultures and current concerns.

THE COUNCIL OF TRENT

A particular reference point for the *General Instruction,* and the Missal itself, is the Council of Trent. The introduction to the GIRM is concerned in part with the relationship between the norms of the Council of Trent and the reforms stemming from Vatican II. We can begin this exploration by noting the ways in which our document understands itself to be in continuity with Trent and the initiatives that flowed from it. The *Instruction* sets out that both reforms share a similar aim of the further integration of the faithful into the liturgy:

> *...the liturgical norms of the Council of Trent have certainly been complemented and perfected in many respects by those of the Second Vatican Council, which has brought to realization the efforts of the last four hundred years to bring the faithful closer to the sacred Liturgy especially in recent times, and above all the zeal for the Liturgy promoted by Saint Pius X and his successors.* (15)

As well, the two conciliar movements are seen to have used a common process for reform. Both are said to have embraced the same tradition, introducing changes and restoring practices in light of the "ancient norm of the Fathers." The *Instruction* warns that differences on the surface level between the current Roman Missal and that of Pius V do not make up the full picture: *Furthermore, if the inner elements of this tradition are reflected upon, it also becomes clear how outstandingly and felicitously the older Roman Missal is brought to fulfillment in the new* (6). Alongside the sharing of a common tradition, both reforms are described as being moved by the same spirit and pastoral concern (14) and as attentive to the pedagogic and pastoral character of the liturgy (12).

This unity in aim and method is enhanced by a common desire to uphold particular traditions, namely, the sacrificial nature of the Mass (2), the ministerial priesthood (4), and the real presence of Christ under the eucharistic species (3). The *Instruction* understands these three as important concerns of Pius V as he put into practice the norms of Trent. It also describes them as "more recent" traditions, under attack from the theologians of the Reformation (7). The GIRM does not elaborate on the meaning of "more recent," however, its sense appears to be that the Council of Trent keenly upheld the medieval formulation of these three questions. The *Institutio,* too, has maintained a close connection with the medieval formulations, and so with the concerns of Trent. It will be interesting, however, to see how these issues are developed as more of the patristic heritage is brought to bear on the three questions (8).

According to the *Instruction,* the current Roman Missal brings about the completion and perfection of norms from Trent that were not received or implemented. Councils and reforms can be resisted. The three mentioned are the restoration of the homily on Sundays and Holy Days of Obligation, the permission to interpose some remarks at appropriate places during the liturgy, and participation in Communion by the faithful at each Mass (13). Yet the tridentine influence is not always so helpful. We will discuss in a later chapter the tension between the two understandings of the priest in the document. It can also be said that the restrictions around Communion under both kinds remain overly concerned with providing a defense of the teaching of Trent that Christ, whole and entire, is received under only one species (281–83).

Clearly there are differences between the current Roman Missal and that of Pius V after the Council of Trent. The reintroduction of the vernacular, the sign of peace, and the general intercessions signal major shifts. The variety of Eucharistic Prayers, with their acclamations, has opened up our eucharistic thinking and praying. Occasionally, there are numbers that explicitly halt a common tridentine practice, such as the admonition that there is only one collect, prayer over the offerings, and post-Communion prayer to be used in a Mass (54, 77, 89). Our aim here, however, has been to show how the *Instruction* sets out the continuity between the reforms of Vatican II and those of the Council of Trent.

UNITY

Along with the theology of tradition, the *General Instruction* focuses a great deal on the theme of unity. It does so in a variety of ways, each somewhat different but all interconnected. Of major interest in the document is the question of the unity of the church in the Eucharist itself. The celebration of the eucharistic liturgy ought to manifest the unity of the particular churches with the church universal. This is to be seen in the unity of doctrine, of sacramental signs, and of practices that are universal in the church through apostolic and unbroken tradition (397). While it is not always clear what the *Instruction* understands by the universal church, the need for unity across the diverse churches is an absolute.[1] Unity among the various churches includes a unity in eucharistic celebration throughout the history of the church itself. This is evident in the discussion of the liturgy of the word where the scriptural readings are understood as the word of God addressed to all people of every era (29). Similarly, in the discussion of the liturgy of the Eucharist, the sacrificial meal instituted by Jesus is spoken of in terms of being continuously made present in the church (72). To enter the liturgy of the Mass, then, is to be one in an action celebrated across the world and throughout the history of the church.

In particular, the *Instruction* is concerned with the Roman Rite. The Roman Missal is put forward, along with the other approved rites, as forming the identity and unitary expression of the Roman Rite. Consequently, the promulgation and publication of the Missal are to be closely overseen by the Church of Rome (397). The Missal is also understood as a guarantee of future unity, as conveyed in the final paragraph of the *Instruction: And so, the Roman Missal, even if in different languages and with some variety of customs, must be preserved in the future as an instrument and an outstanding sign of the integrity and unity of the Roman Rite* (399). Although this is currently the case, and the *Instruction* states it unambiguously, history offers some pause for further reflection. The Roman Church has survived well for almost its entire existence with a variety of Missals. The ancient city of Rome itself had a tradition of different Missals across the city. The *Instruction*'s claim that the Roman Rite has incorporated into itself a variety of usages is certainly true. It is not so clear whether that points to a process of organic and harmonious growth (397). Other factors could well have been involved. Further, it remains to be asked whether this incorporation of outside usages means that the Roman Rite has acquired "a certain supraregional character" (397) so that there is no need for new families of rites (398). It remains an open question whether the unity of the Catholic Church is so closely tied to continued usage of the current Roman Missal.

The GIRM takes up a further aspect of ecclesial unity. The Mass is seen as the outstanding act of the unity of the diocese: *The Eucharistic celebration is an action of Christ and the Church, namely, the holy people united and ordered under the Bishop* (91). Each Eucharist is an action that forges the unity of the local church.

How is unity reflected within the celebration itself? There are a number of ways in which the *Instruction* encourages unity within the assembly. When addressing the lay faithful, it reminds them that their participation should be marked by unity in charity, the avoidance of all individualism, and the recognition that all are brothers and sisters (95). Each Mass is celebrated by a single assembly, the people of God gathered with a priest presiding (27). The unity of all present is to be achieved through participation in the dialogues, the acclamations (34, 35), and singing (39, 40, 47). Uniformity of posture is given special prominence as a source of unity. We can see this in two excerpts from one paragraph:

> *The gestures and postures of the priest, the deacon, and the ministers, as well as those of the people, ought to contribute to making the entire celebration resplendent with beauty and noble simplicity...A common posture, to be observed by all participants, is a sign of the unity of the members of the Christian community gathered for the sacred Liturgy: it both expresses and fosters the intention and spiritual attitude of the participants.* (42)

A number of points emerge from this excerpt. Postures are not considered private actions but part of the making of the liturgy. The range of postures is seen to draw the liturgy as a whole together, and contributes significantly to its aesthetic appeal. As well, uniformity of posture manifests the unity of the assembly, a point reinforced later in the *Instruction: This unity is beautifully apparent from the gestures and postures observed in common by the faithful* (96). Unity through posture requires a degree of willing ritual obedience. The gestures and postures of the members of the assembly, ordained and lay faithful, are not a question of private inclination or arbitrary choice. Rather, they are related to the directives of the *Instruction* and the traditional practices of the Roman Rite, in light of the pastoral orientation that comes from being attentive to the common spiritual good of the faithful (42). These form the criteria for the directive that the faithful should follow the directions given by the deacon, lay minister, or priest (43).

The theme of the unity of the assembly is also evident in discussions about presiding and ministries. While the *Instruction* allows for a number of ministers to share the different parts of that ministry (109), there can be only one presiding celebrant who must exercise all the parts of the office of presiding (108). As well, once the Mass has begun no priest can be admitted to the liturgy as a concelebrant

(206). Concelebration is understood as an appropriate expression of the unity of the priesthood, of the sacrifice, and of the whole people of God (199). The *Instruction* also takes care to avoid the position and posture of concelebrants interrupting the unity of the assembly as a whole, and obscuring the sacred action from the sight and prayer of the lay faithful (215).

Paragraph 162 offers an intriguing challenge with regard to the unity of the assembly. It teaches that the priest may be assisted in the distribution of Communion by other priests "who happen to be present." What does *present* mean in this case? Many communities have become used to the practice of priests who have not been participating in the celebration appearing from the sacristy simply to help out with Communion. Yet this does little to build up the unity of the assembly, and, on reflection, runs counter to the integrity of the gathered community. It is difficult to see that waiting in the sacristy is a form of participation. Consequently, it can be asked whether the practice should continue, especially given the provision for extraordinary ministers and the like in the number itself.

Within the Mass there are a number of rites that reflect different aspects of unity. The *Instruction* insists on the unity of the liturgy as a whole, describing it as a single table of word and sacrament that provides us with instruction and refreshment (28). The unity of the assembly is said to be intensified in the opening rites (46) and the profession of faith (67). This unity is seen to be extended beyond the community gathered to the whole church and to the whole human family in the General Intercessions (69) and the sign of peace (82). Attentiveness to the word of God is related to the encouragement of the Holy Spirit in our hearts (56). In the reception of Holy Communion there is union with Christ and with each other in Christ. These are given particular emphasis in the Communion song and procession (86).

The church building too should reflect the unity of the assembly at worship: *All these elements, even though they must express the hierarchical structure and the diversity of*

31

ministries, should nevertheless bring about a close and coherent unity that is clearly expressive of the unity of the entire holy people (294). Even the statues and images should reflect the devotion of the entire community (318).

SYMBOL

The *Instruction* taps into the rich vein of symbols that composes Roman liturgy. It is impossible not to. At the same time there are serious concerns about the adequacy of the understanding of symbol that the GIRM puts forward. There are also questions of whether the symbolic import of some of the rites is given due respect.

The rites within the Mass are seen to be symbolic in that they allow the church to be made manifest and enable faith to come to expression. The dialogues between priest and people, as well as the acclamations, are described in this light: *in fact, they are not simply outward signs of communal celebration but foster and bring about communion between priest and people* (34). Similarly, postures are understood as symbols in that they express faith: *[a common posture] both expresses and fosters the intention and spiritual attitude of the participants* (42). More significantly, the GIRM teaches that the church is given its preeminent expression at a Eucharist in which the bishop presides with a full complement of presbyters, deacons, and lay ministers, and where there is full and active participation of all (112). Most significantly of all, the Mass is the sacramental memorial of the eucharistic sacrifice of the Lord, in which he becomes present in four distinct modes (27). Here we have symbol at its most profound level.

Within the liturgy and the church building there is an array of symbols and signs. According to the *Instruction,* the priest's chair is a symbol of his office of presiding and directing prayer (310). Similarly the diversity of vestments is a symbol of the various offices (335). There is to be only a single altar in each church as a sign of the one Christ and the one Eucharist of the church (303). The tabernacle may not be on an altar at which Mass is celebrated, in keeping with the sign (315). Our list is but a sample of the many levels of symbol and sign described by the *Institutio*.

Although the liturgy is thoroughly caught up in the symbolic, it is important to ask, What theology of symbol is operative in the *Instruction?* Again, the GIRM was not written as a theological treatise. Nevertheless, its treatment of symbol is quite weak. The understanding of the sign value of the rites is laid out in the following paragraph:

> *Because, however, the celebration of the Eucharist, like the entire Liturgy, is carried out through perceptible signs that nourish, strengthen, and express faith, the utmost care must be taken to choose and to arrange those forms and elements set forth by the Church that, in view of the circumstances of the people and the place, will more effectively foster active and full participation and more properly respond to the spiritual needs of the faithful.* (20)

This section is based on the Constitution of the Sacred Liturgy 59. In its time this was a groundbreaking number. It affirmed the teaching that sacraments confer grace. However, it went beyond any presumption that this grace was received "automatically," so to speak, by simply being present at a rite. Rather, the council fathers challenged celebrant and faithful alike to celebrate the sacraments in such a way that participation in the ritual brought about conversion in the participants, expressed their relationship to God, and made manifest the divine love: *They [the sacraments] do indeed impart grace, but, in addition, the very act of celebrating them disposes the faithful most effectively to receive this grace in a fruitful manner, to worship God duly, and to practise charity* (SC 59).

We can feel here the tension between two very different understandings of sacraments and grace. The need to assert that sacraments confer grace reflects the overriding medieval and tridentine concern for the efficacious nature of the sacraments, almost regardless of their actual manner of celebration. From this perspective it is too easy to see the rites and symbols as simply external signs of something that is guaranteed because it has been done validly. It is then possible to consider that the signs may or may not be intrinsic to the sacrament itself. The importance of the signs can be reduced to the fact that they are considered the required vehicles that God and the church have set for proper enactment of the sacrament. Medieval and tridentine theology is much richer than this thumbnail sketch, and we are offering here only the core principle in its most stark reading. Unfortunately, it is not difficult to find examples where the celebration of the rite is sidelined or denigrated by ministers whose main concern is reduced to validity alone.

The insistence on fruitful celebration of the sacraments echoes a more patristic viewpoint in which the sacraments are an experience of the paschal mystery itself. This ancient approach demands that the ritual forms be taken seriously because it is through them that the liturgy is the deepest manifestation of the Body of Christ and a foretaste of the reign of God. From this perspective it is clear that the celebration of the liturgy requires a liturgically literate community, marked both by full, conscious, and active participation, and by a spirit of ongoing conversion (SC 11). This is in line with contemporary theological discussion about symbol, where reality and truth are only known to us in and through the symbols that mediate them.[2] Consequently, symbols are not just vehicles for an abstract truth, but inevitably bring it to us in a particular shape and form since reality cannot be known apart from the symbols that mediate it. In light of this, we can see that the ritual forms of our worship are not peripheral to our understanding of faith, church, and salvation, but are an integral part of it.

Almost forty years after the promulgation of the Constitution on the Sacred Liturgy the 2002 *General Instruction* remains caught between these two approaches.

It highly values ritual participation (20, 34, 42). Further, in a discussion of Communion under both kinds the *Instruction* shows the understanding that when the sacramental sign is clear, then the people can enter the mystery it points to: *...the Council thus gave permission for the reception of Communion under both kinds on some occasions, because this clearer form of the sacramental sign offers a particular opportunity of deepening the understanding of the mystery in which the faithful take part* (14). Yet even here we glimpse the tentativeness of its approach. There is some stress on the importance of understanding the liturgy, especially through the use of the vernacular (12, 13).

What then is missing? On a number of occasions the *Instruction* clouds or inhibits the power of key eucharistic symbols. I would like to offer a range of examples of this. One set of points is around the gifts of bread and wine, the offerings. In a rather optimistic turn of phrase, the *Instruction* tries to overcome the fact that the faithful feel almost no identification with the bread and wine that are used in the Mass: *Even though the faithful no longer bring from their own possessions the bread and wine intended for the liturgy as in the past, nevertheless the rite of carrying up the offerings still retains its force and its spiritual significance* (73). This is very difficult to defend. First, there is no requirement that there be a procession of the gifts, though that is described as praiseworthy. Second, how do the people actually identify with the bread and wine if the regular practice is the withholding of the cup and the distribution of Communion from hosts reserved in the tabernacle? Third, the ancient practice was not focused on the procession, as there probably was no formal procession of the gifts. Rather, it was focused on the fact that the bread and wine for the Lord's table came from the tables of the faithful—bishop included—as did any offerings for the poor and the church. It was immediately identifiable as their food and drink, and as their food and drink was worthy to be transformed into the food of eternal life. The *Instruction* makes a valiant plea that the bread actually look something like food, and that it be large enough for breaking and sharing, as in apostolic times:

> *The meaning of the sign demands that the material for the Eucharistic celebration truly have the appearance of food. It is therefore expedient that the Eucharistic bread, even though unleavened and baked in the traditional shape, be made in such a way that the priest at Mass with a congregation is able in practice to break it into parts for distribution to at least some of the faithful.* (321)

We can see that the primary symbol of bread and wine—as the food of the people, provided by the people, broken and shared with the people, and available for the poor—is greatly inhibited. The concern, rather, is for the later disciplines of the use of unleavened bread and the centrality of the priest's Communion. Today virtually no community in the Western Church can provide its own bread for the liturgy, with most of it shipped across countries and oceans from specialized bakeries. Rarely is it "recently baked" (320). The primary eucharistic symbol of the bread and wine is inhibited by secondary considerations.

The same can be seen with regard to the rite of peace and the rite of Communion. The rite of peace has two aspects, the prayer for peace and the exchange of a sign of peace: *The Rite of Peace follows, by which the Church asks for peace and unity for herself and for the whole human family, and the faithful express to each other their ecclesial communion and mutual charity before communicating in the Sacrament* (82). It is not clear from this whether the "faithful" refers only to the lay faithful or includes all members of the assembly. The actual description of the rite (154) puts the emphasis on the prayer rather than on the sign itself. It describes the prayer and the greeting. However, the priest celebrant may issue the invitation to exchange the sign of peace "when appropriate" (154). When the peace is offered, the celebrant offers the sign of peace to the concelebrants who are near him (239), and then to a deacon if present (181). Moreover, neither priest, concelebrant, or deacon is obliged to exchange the sign of peace with the nonordained ministers at the altar. Nor ought the priest leave the sanctuary, in case the celebration be disturbed (154). Moreover, the lay faithful are admonished to offer the sign of peace only to those who are nearby (82). While the description of the rite in the 2002 GIRM is more open than that in the 1975 GIRM, it has not kept pace with customary practice. Our focus here is on the understanding of operative symbol. The emphasis in the *Instruction* continues to fall on the prayer and not on the actual sign. The sign is made optional, and the laity is fenced off from the ordained if the exchange takes place. We can see here that the *Instruction* exhibits a preference for words over actions, and that it is more concerned with the preservation of hierarchical boundaries than with giving concrete form to the deeper unity of the members of Christ's body. At the same time, the sign is described as an expression of ecclesial communion and mutual charity (82), manifesting peace, communion, and charity (154). As we have it now the sign of peace is a significant gesture whose profound evangelical and symbolic import is restricted for theological and rubrical concerns.

Similar points can be made with regard to the rite of Communion. The *Instruction* is insistent on the separation of the priest's Communion from that of the lay faithful. The priest communes in both the Body and Blood of Christ consecrated at that Mass, but not necessarily the lay faithful (85). Extraordinary ministers of Communion are not to approach the altar before the priest's Communion, and should always accept the vessel from which they will distribute Communion from the hands of the priest (162). The Communion antiphon can be inserted between the priest's Communion and that of the faithful (87). Efforts are made to bring unity to the rite. The Communion song is to be sung from the priest's reception of Communion for as long as the faithful are still coming forward as an expression of the communicant's union in spirit and the communitarian nature of the procession (86). It is seen as desirable that the faithful receive the Lord's Body from hosts consecrated at that Mass (85). It seems quite sad, and only too human, that the high point of unity between each member of the assembly in and with Christ and each other is saddled by concerns for hierarchical order and separation.

In light of this, there is probably little need to expand on the reluctance within the Roman Rite for the laity to partake in the Blood of Christ. Beyond the dated polemics of the Reformation, it is difficult to defend the restrictions around Communion under both kinds. Jesus himself distributed bread and cup at the Last Supper, and our celebration of the eucharistic rite in the Mass is said to correspond to his actions: *Accordingly, the Church has arranged the entire celebration of the Liturgy of the Eucharist in parts corresponding to precisely these words and actions of Christ* (72). As with the cases above, our practices and their underpinning theologies work to inhibit our rites being fully signs and symbols of the heavenly realities.

It is worth offering a taste of what will be treated more fully in chapter 4 about the theologies of priesthood in the *Instruction*. The patristic theology of priesthood concentrates on the role of the *sacerdos* in his oversight of the whole celebration. It is attentive to the pastoral situation and needs of the assembly, the genres and forms within the rite, and appropriate consultation. This approach respects and explores the symbolic nature of the liturgy. The other theological stream, built around a theology of the priest acting in the person of Christ, offers a clear interpretation of how the Mass can be an action of Christ, with an overriding emphasis on validity and efficacy. In such a theology the participation of all other members of the assembly—deacons, ministers, and lay faithful—is considered important but not actually necessary. As such, the symbolic dimension of the liturgy is severely inhibited.

In summary, we can see that the *General Instruction* upholds the symbols within the liturgy and calls for greater participation in them. The understanding of symbol itself, however, is not quite adequate to this task, reflecting few of the changes in scholarship and patristic studies over the past forty years. This may well be due in part to a disproportionate amount of attention to questions of efficacy, validity, hierarchical order, and sixteenth-century Reformation polemics—much to the detriment of our expression of the symbol that the Eucharist is.

LEX ORANDI LEX CREDENDI

What does the *Instruction* say about the relationship of liturgy to doctrine, usually expressed through the Latin tag *lex orandi lex credendi?* The *lex orandi* corresponds to our worship, while the *lex credendi* refers to the teachings of faith.

On the occasions that the GIRM takes up the issue directly, it places worship at the service of doctrine. It understands that the church's rule of prayer ought to correspond to its perennial rule of belief (2). The Roman Missal, as a book of prayers, clearly is seen as a witness to the rule of prayer. At the same time, however, it is to be a guardian of the deposit of faith: *The new Missal, therefore, while bearing witness to the Roman Church's rule of prayer (lex orandi), also safeguards the deposit of faith handed down by the more recent Councils and marks in its own right a step of great importance in liturgical tradition* (10). We can see here something of a problem. No one wants to deny that worship reflects teaching, or that our doctrine needs to influence the shape and content of our prayers. It is important to realize, though, that the deposit of faith is much more than the sum of doctrinal statements. As well, it is not always so clear, first, what is exactly meant by the "deposit of faith handed down by the more recent Councils," and second, whether these more recent understandings are actually reflected in the ancient prayers and rites preserved by the Missal. It could well be asked whether the more ancient formulations and rites offer a critique and corrective of practices, tendencies, and theologies from the second millennium. Here the law of prayer would be a guide in the law of belief. This also provides an indication as to the need, well expressed in the *Instruction,* to continue broad exploration of the norms of the fathers (8, 9). A later paragraph in the *Institutio* is more felicitous. When referring to the integrity of the faith, it speaks of doctrines of the faith, sacramental signs, and apostolic, unbroken usages that are in accord with both particular churches and the universal church (397). Here we have a more dynamic sense of the deposit of faith, one that includes the robust unity amid the diversity of liturgical practices across the variety of churches in accordance with scriptural and apostolic warrant.

At other times the *Instruction* makes us aware that liturgy is more than an exemplar of church teaching. It is an expression of the very mystery of the church, the sanctification of the world by God, and our response in Christ (16). Our prayers and rites are not statements of belief but proclamations and songs of faith (392). The prefaces within the Eucharistic Prayer are described as expressions of thanksgiving that reveal different facets of the mystery of salvation (364). The Mass is that sacrificial meal in which the sacrifice of the cross is continuously made present in the church (72). The *lex orandi* of the church is much more than a grounds for expressing teachings. In fact, the original and enduring meaning of orthodoxy is "right praise," that is, right worship, before it is "correct teaching." From this perspective we can ask whether the symbols and rites of the liturgy have always been well served by formulations of church teaching and theology.

In effect, the *General Instruction* reflects two opposing approaches.[3] The original fifth-century adage was explicit that the law of prayer governed the law of belief: *Legem credendi lex statuat supplicandi.* The law of prayer, however, was not reduced to the content of prayers. The law of prayer had three levels. First, it had to be based in scripture. Second, it had to be attested to by practice across the churches. Only then, third, could the content of prayers be examined for their theological value. It was in this way that the living tradition of prayer had something to offer the development and formulation of doctrine. In contemporary times, most noticeably under Pius XII in his encyclical *Mediator Dei* (1947), the original sense has been diminished. The saying has come to mean that dogma is the source of liturgy, and that liturgy learns from dogma rather than offers it insights from the living tradition. The *Instruction* contains elements of the ancient tradition and the modern Roman curial position. Overtly, we read that liturgy is subject to dogma. However, since the Eucharist is also described as the center of the whole of Christian life (16), the GIRM opens up the deposit of faith beyond formularies and dogmas into life in the triune God.

CONCLUSION

The more that we can have a handle on the range of theological issues and positions within the *General Instruction* the more we are able to engage with it, appreciate its strengths, and go beyond its shortfalls. Further, by examining what it means by tradition, unity, symbol, and doctrine we are able to outline some of the different avenues of thought that contribute to the *Institutio*. As much as it is a single document, it is not necessarily a single work, already having gone through a number of editions and countless committees. In this it simply mirrors all our major church writings, and indeed the Roman Missal itself. As part of the ongoing liturgical tradition we need to be open to the insights and possibilities that the *General Instruction* offers. At the same time, we are obliged to bring to it our lived experience and theological considerations so that what comes through is the mystery of salvation alive and active in our world. That is traditional worship.

CHAPTER THREE
THE MYSTERY
OF THE CHURCH

In celebrations at which the Bishop presides, and especially in the celebration of the Eucharist led by the Bishop himself with the presbyterate, the deacons, and the people taking part, the mystery of the Church is revealed. (22)

The celebration of the Eucharist reveals the mystery of the church. The absolute centrality of this point can be too easily lost amid the details, instructions, adaptations, and exhortations that make up the *General Instruction*. Yet it remains that the celebration of the Eucharist is the manifestation of the church.

The *Instruction* does not offer a comprehensive theology of the church; nevertheless, it continually refers to the church in theological, practical, and legislative terms. We are left with the task of asking how the document understands the term *church*. What is the range of meanings it brings to this word and how do they fit together? We will begin with the more theological aspects and conclude with an examination of the church as an institutional structure.

THE THEOLOGY OF THE CHURCH

It is no easy task to capture the various strands of the theology of church in the *Instruction*. Some are biblical, with strong references to the New Testament. Others can be classified as referring to the apostolic nature of the church. There are elements of the church as a foretaste of the reign of God. As well, there is the understanding of the church as hierarchy. Our challenge is that these theological understandings remain underdeveloped throughout the document yet at the same time are used to underpin the theology and practice of the *Institutio.* It is an interesting dynamic. The approach taken here is to identify the images, explore their sense from the point of view of the scriptures and theology, and then ask how well or how poorly the metaphors are used in the GIRM.

BIBLICAL IMAGERY OF THE CHURCH

Four biblical images are at work in the *General Instruction,* providing the foundation for consequent developments. They are not set down in any particular order. Rather, they sit alongside one another adding layers of richness and variety. The four are the church as the bride of Christ, the holy people of God, the body, and the baptized.

THE BRIDE OF CHRIST

We meet the bridal metaphor very early. Repeating paragraph 47 from the Constitution on the Sacred Liturgy, the *General Instruction* describes the church as the "beloved bride," who has been entrusted by Christ with the memorial of his sacrifice on the cross until he returns (2). In the Letter to the Ephesians the nuptial imagery is used to give a sense of Christ's love for the church. The headship of Christ over the church is obviously, if now somewhat clumsily, stated: *For the husband is the head of the wife just as Christ is head of the church, the body of which he is the saviour* (Eph 5:23). It is the second part of the sentence that is most important for us. Christ is head of the church because out of love he brought salvation. The sense is made more clear a little later, though the husband inference is a distraction:

> *Husbands, love your wives, just as Christ loved the church and gave himself up for her, in order to make her holy by cleansing her with the washing of water by the word, so as to present the church to himself in splendour, without spot or wrinkle or anything of that kind – yes, so that she may be holy and without blemish.* (Eph 5:25–27; 2 Cor 11:2)

From the scripture we can see that the church is only "bride" in and through the love of Christ and his saving death. The holiness of the church is from Christ. The intimacy of the church with Christ comes from Christ. The cleansing of the church is effective because it is an act of the word. Returning then to the *General Instruction,* we can see that the church, as bride, can be entrusted with the memorial of the cross only because Christ remains so close to and true to it. The image of the church as bride says more about Christ than about the church and reminds us that it must always be Christ who is at the center of every sense of the church.

There is a second bridal image in the New Testament referred to somewhat obliquely in the GIRM. When dealing with sacred images, the *Instruction* speaks of the church journeying toward the heavenly liturgy celebrated in the holy city of Jerusalem (318). Here the allusion is to the Book of Revelation: *And I saw the holy city, the new Jerusalem, coming down out of heaven from God, prepared as a bride adorned for her husband* (Rev 21:2). The bridal reference is slight, but comes into play in our discussion later in this chapter of the church as the foretaste of the fulfillment of the reign of God.

THE HOLY PEOPLE OF GOD

More common throughout the *Instruction* than the bridal metaphor is the image of the church as the people of God, particularly the holy people of God. The preferred term in the Constitution on the Sacred Liturgy is the *Christian people*.[1] Yet only a year later in the Second Vatican Council's Dogmatic Constitution on the Church, the designation "people of God" becomes the primary interpretation of the mystery of the church. There, the whole of chapter 2 is devoted to it, and only then comes the exposition of the hierarchical nature of the church (chapter 3). The *Instruction* reflects this shift in the Council documents.

Scripturally the phrase is found most explicitly in the First Letter of Peter:

> But you are a chosen race, a royal priesthood, a holy nation, God's own people, in order that you may proclaim the mighty acts of him who called you out of darkness into his marvellous light. Once you were not a people, but now you are God's people; once you had not received mercy, but now you have received mercy. (1 Pet 2:9–10)

As in the bridal imagery the initiative is God's. The church is chosen, royal, and holy entirely because of the action of God's mercy. There is a wonderful ironic play of ideas in the two verses. The church is not a race, yet this profusion of ethnicities and language groups is made into a chosen race. The community are not priests by any standards of first-century Judaism or the religious world of the Roman Empire. Yet because Christ is in them they are the highest form of priesthood, with the kingly and sacerdotal roles united into a royal priesthood. The baptized are not a nation, but these odd groupings of believers feel themselves to be a single united people, a nation in God. What gives them their cohesion is the mercy freely bestowed on them that brought them from darkness to light. A surface reading of the passage leaves the author of 1 Peter open to the charge of elitism and smugness. That would be a sad reading. It is God who has done the choosing. God chose not on the basis of merit; rather, the mercy of God shed light on sinners confined to the darkness. There is little to be smug about there. Membership of God's holy people does not imply entry into the elite. In fact, it demands the embracing of the divine mission to proclaim the mighty acts of God. The key to living as a member of this people is to bring to the world that undeserved, freely given, and fully forgiving mercy of God. At the same time it calls for continuing conversion: *let yourselves be built into a spiritual house, to be a holy priesthood, to offer spiritual sacrifices acceptable to God through Jesus Christ* (1 Pet 2:5). The author has overturned the accepted canons of race, priesthood, nationhood, and divine treatment of sinners to emphasize the radical transformation of all things when they are in Christ.

Though the *Instruction* takes up this seminal image, its use of it is reserved and a little confusing. At times *people of God* refers to the entire church, as seen in this quotation:

> The Eucharistic celebration is an action of Christ and the Church, namely, the holy people united and ordered under the Bishop. It therefore pertains to the whole Body of the Church, manifests it, and has its effect upon it. It also affects the individual members of the Church in different ways, according to their different orders, offices, and actual participation. In this way, the Christian people, "a chosen race, a royal priesthood, a holy nation, God's own people," expresses its cohesion and its hierarchical ordering. (91)

This excerpt repeats the phrases from the First Letter of Peter. It forcefully reminds the reader of the action of Christ himself. It also makes an interesting connection between the image of the holy people and that of the body, something we shall take up below. Yet it also complements the metaphor with governance: the holy people as united under the bishop. As well, it adds the hierarchical framework of orders and offices. While it is to be expected that the *Instruction* will set these various theological positions side by side it must be asked whether the radical nature of this scriptural understanding of the church has not been somewhat compromised. A similar approach is found earlier in the *Instruction,* where the celebration of the Mass is described as an action of Christ and the people of God arrayed hierarchically (16).

At other times *people of God* is specifically applied to the lay faithful. It is clearest in one of the most eloquent passages of the *Instruction*. The apposite section reads:

> For this people is the People of God, purchased by Christ's Blood, gathered together by the Lord, nourished by his word. It is a people called to bring to God the prayers of the entire human family, a people giving thanks in Christ for the mystery of salvation by offering his Sacrifice. Finally, it is a people made one by sharing in the Communion of Christ's Body and Blood. Though holy in its origins, this people nevertheless grows continually in holiness by its conscious, active, and fruitful participation in the mystery of the Eucharist. (5)

Here we can recognize major themes from the First Letter of Peter: holiness, God's mercy, the mighty deeds achieved in Christ, a priestly and united people. Some of the same understanding is applied to the instructions concerning the prayers of the faithful, where the offering of the intercessions is described as an act of the people exercising their baptismal priesthood (69). Why, then, are such exciting concepts singularly applied to the laity rather than to the community as a whole?

Both paragraphs (5, 69) reflect the pervasive tension in the *General Instruction* between two understandings of priesthood: the scriptural view of the church as a royal priesthood and the ministerial priesthood of the ordained within the hierarchical order. This extended extract from paragraph 5 follows on from the discussion in previous paragraphs of the nature of the ministerial priesthood proper to a bishop and a priest. The eloquence of the paragraph is partly due to the recognition that the "priesthood of the people" ought to be highly regarded, and that the contribution of the lay faithful to the celebration has been neglected in the course of time.

The image of the people of God is assigned to the faithful as distinct from the ordained in paragraph 95. Preceding paragraphs deal with the duties of the ordained ministries of bishop, priest, and deacon. Paragraph 95 begins the section on the functions of the people of God. The opening sentence sets a paraphrase of the verses from 1 Peter within the context of a different theology of priesthood. It reads:

> *In the celebration of Mass the faithful form a holy people, a people whom God has made his own, a royal priesthood, so that they may give thanks to God and offer the spotless Victim not only through the hands of the priest but also together with him, and so that they may learn to offer themselves.* (95)

We will look at how the *Instruction* handles this tension below. It is important to note here that the image of the church as the holy people of God is applied in a mixed fashion. We should be very cautious of reducing the theology of the church as "a chosen race, a royal priesthood, a holy nation, God's own people" to just "the lay faithful." The danger is that the ordained ministry can be seen as outside of and over this church, rather than a part of it.

Before continuing onto the image of the church as body a comment is required about language. The *Instruction* has had to find some way of speaking about ministers, ordained and lay. In doing so, it uses a variety of terms to describe those who are not ministers but make up the gathering. The word *people* is regularly used as a synonym for the members of the congregation. Another term is the *lay faithful*. While this is more a problem of liturgical language and the limits of our technical vocabulary in both Latin and the vernacular, it can unintentionally reinforce any current division between the lay faithful and the ordained.

THE BODY

There appear to be two overtly scriptural metaphors of the church as body used in the *General Instruction*. Both take their origin from the First Letter to the Corinthians. Not surprisingly, Paul's image of the church as the body of Christ is used to appreciate the unity and complementarity of the various ministries and functions in the liturgy. Writing to the Corinthians about gifts leads Paul to meditate on the diversity among the members in the church (1 Cor 12–13). They come from different races, classes, and genders, and bring different characteristics and gifts. They belong because God has called them and they have been baptized into the one Spirit. They are so united that what affects one affects all. All members have their place, and God has arranged it so that no member is less deserving or less worthy of respect. Ultimately all gifts, roles, deeds of power, forms of assistance, and the like are secondary, passing, and partial when compared to the gifts that abide: faith, hope, and most importantly love, the greatest of them all.

For Paul's hearers in Corinth there was a startling novelty in what he was presenting to them. They were accustomed to the analogy of the body as a justification for all manner of inequalities, along the lines that if the upper classes were content (the more important parts of the body), then they would ensure that all others were content (the lesser parts). The key was that all remain in their place in the hierarchy of the empire. For Paul, the body of Christ ought to know nothing of this.

The *Instruction* alludes to this passage at least twice. The first is the most explicit. The section on sacred vestments commences with it: *In the Church, which is the Body of Christ, not all members have the same office* (335). The text then goes on to detail how the vestments are to reflect the variety of offices in the celebration of the liturgy. The metaphor is put to similar use in an earlier chapter on the duties and ministries in the Mass (91). We have already examined this particular passage for the way it speaks of the church as the people of God. Here the reference is to the body of the church but the sense is the same as the church, the body of Christ. Again it forms part of the opening paragraph of the chapter: ...*It therefore pertains to the whole Body of the Church, manifests it, and has its effect upon it. It also affects the individual members of the Church in different ways, according to their different orders, offices, and actual participation* (91).

This metaphor of the body is adapted by the *Instruction* in support of the liturgical reform and the mutual responsibilities among the members of the celebrating assembly. The sacred action is celebrated necessarily with a variety of ministers and ministries. None is more worthy, though they are not all the same. They require different gifts. The participation of all is a requisite. There should be no appearance of individualism or division, a point applied to the laity (95). Indeed the lay faithful should be willing to take up responsibility when required (96). At the same time, we see that the image of the body of Christ prefaces instructions and decisions reflecting the hierarchical ordering of ministries and the church itself. Again there is a tension here. The body of Christ as found in 1 Corinthians does not support hierarchy as such, but it does call for a church that is cohesive, gifted, generous, reliant on God, and appreciative of the belonging and contribution of each member. It has something of the feel of the parable of the widow's mite about it (Mark 12:41–44).

On the other hand, when this image is applied to hierarchical order, as it is in the GIRM, it necessarily applies to our structures principles that challenge any complacency. The body of Christ as hierarchically ordered should not be just any type of political structure.

The *Instruction* is also sensitive to the pastoral dimension of the unity of the body. Reminiscent of the injunction that when one member of the body suffers all suffer, the image of the church as Christ's body is called on in the discussion of Masses for the Dead: *The Church offers the Eucharistic Sacrifice of Christ's Passover for the dead so that, since all the members of Christ's body are in communion with each other, the petition for spiritual help on behalf of some may bring comforting hope to others* (379).

The *General Instruction* alludes to Paul (1 Cor 10:17), the Last Supper tradition (Matt 26:26–29; Mark 14:22–26; Luke 22:14–23; 1 Cor 11:23–26), and the practices of the first Christian communities (Acts 2:46) when it speaks of the unity of the assembly signified in the action of breaking the bread during the rite of Communion: *Christ's gesture of breaking bread at the Last Supper, which gave the entire Eucharistic Action its name in apostolic times, signifies that the many faithful are made one body (1 Cor 10:17) by receiving Communion from the one Bread of Life which is Christ, who died and rose for the salvation of the world* (83). These references to the Last Supper traditions and the apostolic community point to the action of Christ and the subsequent unity of the church. Paul is concerned with questions of appropriate behavior, particularly right worship and fidelity:

> *Therefore, my dear friends, flee from the worship of idols. I speak as to sensible people; judge for yourselves what I say. The cup of blessing that we bless, is it not a sharing in the blood of Christ? The bread that we break, is it not a sharing in the body of Christ? Because there is one bread, we who are many are one body, for we all partake of the one bread.* (1 Cor 10:14–17)

51

The *Instruction* does not take up the ethical and liturgical context. Rather it uses the scriptural passage to further an appreciation of the work of Christ and the unity of the faithful through Communion. The scriptural excerpt also serves as a reminder that the reception of Communion is not an added extra in the Mass, but an essential part of its divine and apostolic fabric.

BAPTISM

The image of the first Christians as the people who have undergone baptism is foundational for every under-standing of the church. The communities of the New Testament consisted of those who had gone into the grave with Christ and had been raised up with him to newness of life as the adopted children of God (Rom 6–8). Jesus author-ized the church to make disciples of all nations through baptism in the threefold divine name (Matt 28:18–20). Paul's image of the body of Christ is predicated upon baptism: *For in the one Spirit we were all baptised into one body – Jews and Greeks, slaves or free – and we were all made to drink of the one Spirit* (1 Cor 12:13). The First Letter of Peter, with its reminder to the members of the church that they were a royal priesthood, a holy people, is an exposition of their rebirth in Christ. The first act of the Christian life is to undergo baptism, and the whole of the Christian life is to bring that seed to fruit: *You have been born anew, not of perishable but of imperishable seed, through the living and enduring word of God* (1 Pet 2:23). A point that is somewhat lost on us, but which was much clearer in apostolic times, is that baptism is the only initiation a Christian undergoes. Unlike the cults of that time, there were no grades or levels of belonging as a Christian.

Baptism is explicitly invoked in the *General Instruction* in the context of the dignity, rights, and duties of the lay faithful. The dignity of baptism is taken up when dealing with the incensation of the altar during the preparation of the gifts. The *Instruction* reads: *Next, the priest, because of his sacred ministry, and the people, by reason of their baptismal dignity, may be incensed by the deacon or another minister* (75). Ordained and lay are given equal honor; both are incensed with three swings back and forth of the thurible (277). The document refers to the rights and duties of the baptized as central to its insistence on the participation of all in the celebration of the liturgy. While the quotation is rather long, and is taken up elsewhere across the chapter, it is too important to cut short:

> *This will be best accomplished if, with due regard for the nature and the particular circumstances of each liturgical assembly, the entire celebration is planned in such a way that it leads to a conscious, active, and full participation of the faithful both in body and in mind, a participation burning with faith, hope, and charity, of the sort which is desired by the Church and demanded by the very nature of the celebration, and to which the Christian people have a right and duty by reason of their Baptism.* (18, 386)

The paragraph is lifted directly from the Constitution on the Sacred Liturgy (14). The Constitution places the participation of the people at the heart of the renewed liturgy: *full and active participation by all the people...is the primary, indeed the indispensable source from which the faithful are to derive the true Christian spirit* (SC 14). The Vatican Council has offered our worship a great challenge. Outside of this kind of participation how can the church be the church? How can the celebration be true to its nature? How can the baptized live out their baptism?

It would have been interesting to see the *General Instruction* use more broadly the metaphor of the community of the baptized. Nevertheless by applying it directly to the dignity, rights, and duties of the lay faithful in the liturgy it sheds light on the nature of the church in two ways. One is that hierarchy is related to ministry rather than dignity. Can there be a greater dignity than being a child of God and joint heir with Christ? (Rom 8:17) The second is that the church itself is impoverished through any neglect of the rights and duties of the people at worship.

SUMMARY

The *General Instruction* takes up four New Testament images of church. In effect these images present something of a dilemma for the document. Each is rich and greatly enhances the depth of the document. At the same time the application of each in the *Instruction* is limited and, in some cases, strained. The bride is only holy because of the actions of Christ. The people of God are more than the laity. The church as a whole is a royal priesthood. The image of the body defies the norms of unequal power relationships. Baptism is the only context for all church office and belonging, since Christianity knows no other grade or level of initiation. Significantly, the inclusion of these biblical metaphors offers an inbuilt set of criteria for assessing the *Institutio* and its application.

THE CHURCH AS APOSTOLIC

Dispersed throughout the *Instruction* are references back to the time of the apostles. The Dogmatic Constitution on Divine Revelation, *Dei Verbum* (DV) from Vatican II stakes out the grounds for the contemporary official understanding of the sense of *apostolic:*

> *This commission was faithfully fulfilled by the apostles who, by their oral preaching, by example, and by ordinances, handed on what they had received from the lips of Christ, from living with Him, and from what He did, or what they had learned through the prompting of the Holy Spirit.*

The commission was fulfilled, too, by those apostles and apostolic men who under the inspiration of the same Holy Spirit committed the message of salvation to writing. (DV 7)

Fidelity to what was handed on by the apostles is seen to enable the church to remain authentic in doctrine, life, and worship (DV 8). Inseparable from the apostolic tradition are the scriptures. Together they are said to make up the single deposit of the word of God, which is established as the grounds for the unity of the church: *By adhering to it the entire holy people, united to its pastors, remains always faithful to the teaching of the apostles, to the communion of life, to the breaking of bread and the prayers (cf Acts 2:42)* (DV 10). We can see that the word of God, in particular the scriptures and the practices of the apostles, provides for all the members and offices in the church the criteria for what is to be regarded as apostolic. As well, we can see that the Vatican II document on revelation is keenly aware of the place of liturgy in the tradition, referring both to what has come from Christ and from the earliest communities.

The *General Instruction* reflects an apostolic understanding of the church. It is attentive to the example of Christ, to the practices of the first communities, and to the scriptures. Finally, the church is described as the steward and teacher of these aspects of the word of God.

The *Instruction* opens with the example of Christ and its implications for consequent ecclesial practice. Naturally it refers to the Last Supper. The first two sentences read:

When he was about to celebrate with his disciples the Passover meal in which he instituted the sacrifice of his Body and Blood, Christ the Lord gave instructions that a large, furnished upper room should be prepared (Lk 22:12). The Church has always regarded this command as applying also to herself when she gives directions about the preparation of people's hearts and minds and of the

> *places, rites, and texts for the celebration of the*
> *Most Holy Eucharist.* (1)

The eucharistic liturgy in the Mass especially is described as corresponding to the actions and words of Jesus himself. It must be noted that sometimes there is a little embroidering of the scriptural record. The church uses bread and wine as Christ did, though unlike the *General Instruction,* the scriptural record does not specify water: *Following the example of Christ, the Church has always used bread and wine with water to celebrate the Lord's Supper* (319). There are more significant examples. According to the *General Instruction* the Mass makes present the sacrifice on the cross in the church when the church carries out, through the ministry of the priest, what the Lord himself did and handed on to the disciples to do in his memory. This part of the Mass, then, is understood to emerge from the accounts of the Last Supper: *Accordingly the Church has arranged the entire celebration of the Liturgy of the Eucharist in parts corresponding to precisely these words and actions of Christ* (72). Without doubt the Last Supper narratives are the basis here. The "words of Christ" repeated in the Eucharistic Prayers, however, do not correspond precisely to any of the scriptural passages. Rather, they are a liturgical interpretation of that utterly foundational text. The *General Instruction* reads a little defensively on this point. This lack of precise scriptural language does not compromise to any degree the apostolic nature of the liturgy, especially since the memorial is celebrated by the church in fulfillment of Christ's own command (79d, e).

The *General Instruction* reflects the awareness that the church follows not only Christ's instruction but also apostolic practice. An example of this is found when the *Instruction* discusses the duties of the deacon and describes the order as being held in high honor even from the time of the apostles (94).

The church at worship in the Mass can also be understood as apostolic because its action is suffused with the scriptures. At one level we can see this easily with the centrality of the liturgy of the word (28) and the scriptural nature of many of the prayers—the best example being the Lord's Prayer. Yet there is a deeper scriptural foundation, which the *Instruction* describes as follows:

> For it is out of the Sacred Scripture that the readings are read and explained in the homily and that psalms are sung, and it is drawing upon the inspiration and spirit of Sacred Scripture that prayers, orations, and liturgical songs are fashioned in such a way that from them actions and signs derive their meaning. (391)

The importance of this criterion from scripture should not be undervalued. It is taken directly from the Constitution on the Sacred Liturgy (SC 24). Furthermore it was only added to the *General Instruction* in the third edition (2002). This latest edition of the GIRM has introduced a new principle of interpretation from the apostolic nature of the church.

As apostolic, the church is described as teacher and steward, roles that require the wisdom to know when to maintain the course, when to adapt, what to retrieve, and what to create. The church, as teacher of truth, is to be like every scribe trained for the kingdom of heaven in the parable from Matthew's Gospel (Matt 13:52–53). The parable focuses us onto the master of the household, who brings out from his treasure what is new and what is old, a role the GIRM ascribes to the church (15). Later in the *Instruction,* the church is seen as steward with the authority to modify practices when required. The particular reference is to the broadening of the discipline for the reception of Holy Communion beyond the strictures of the Council of Trent. Apostolic stewardship is set out in the following terms:

> *They [sacred pastors] are to teach, furthermore, that the Church, in her stewardship of the Sacraments, has the power to set forth or alter whatever provisions, apart from the substance of the Sacraments, that she judges to be most conducive to the veneration of the Sacraments and the well-being of the recipients, in view of changing conditions, times, and places.* (282)

THE CHURCH AS FORETASTE OF THE REIGN OF GOD

Throughout the *General Instruction* are references to the way in which the church is caught up in the oncoming reign of God. We can marshal these disparate ideas under four groupings: the church in league with the saints in the heavenly liturgy, the church as pilgrim, the church and the poor, and the church as priestly.

THE HEAVENLY LITURGY

It is in the section dealing with the veneration of sacred images that we find an expression of the relationship of the church at worship on earth to the heavenly liturgy. The former is described as a foretaste of the latter:

> *In the earthly Liturgy, the Church participates, by a foretaste, in that heavenly Liturgy which is celebrated in the holy city of Jerusalem toward which she journeys as a pilgrim, and where Christ is sitting at the right hand of God; and by venerating the memory of the Saints, she hopes one day to have some part and fellowship with them.* (318)

This section echoes what is found in the Constitution on the Sacred Liturgy (SC 8) and was inserted for the first time in the 2002 third edition of the GIRM. Behind the quotation is a reference to the Book of Revelation (Rev 21:2), which also contains the image of the church as the perfect bride adorned for her husband. The context in Revelation is the imminent return of Christ, the resurrection of the saints, the renewal of all things, and the unceasing worship of God at the marriage supper of the Lamb (Rev 19–22).

The *General Instruction* takes up this scriptural richness, though somewhat tentatively. It speaks of the need for buildings and their furnishings to be truly worthy and beautiful because they are to be used in divine worship, and so are signs and symbols of heavenly realities (288). When dealing with the rite of Communion, the Eucharist is spoken of in terms of the paschal banquet (80) and the eucharistic banquet (282). This beautiful imagery calls up the marriage supper of the Lamb from the Book of Revelation. It also evokes Jesus' own promise to the disciples in Matthew's narrative of the Last Supper that he would not drink again of the fruit of the vine until he would drink again with them in his Father's kingdom (Matt 26:29).

The importance given to the Sunday parish liturgy points to the fulfillment of all things in Christ. On this point the *Instruction* reads as follows: *Great importance should also be attached to a Mass celebrated with any community, but especially with the parish community, inasmuch as it represents the universal Church gathered at a given time and place. This is particularly true in the communal Sunday celebration* (113). Liturgically and theologically, Sunday is known both as the "first" day, the day of creation, and as the "eighth" day, the first day of the new creation. Implicit in Sunday worship is the revelation of the world remade in Christ. At the same time, the *General Instruction* sees every gathering for the Eucharist as an act of hope in the return of Christ. In particular this is associated with song and joy: *The Christian faithful who gather together as one to await the Lord's coming are instructed by the Apostle Paul to sing together psalms, hymns, and spiritual songs (Col 3:16). Singing is the sign of the heart's joy (Acts 2:46)* (39).

The heavenly liturgy motif is applied more vigorously to the communion among the faithful on earth, the heavenly hosts of angels, and, more so, the saints. The Sanctus is described as a chant sung together with the heavenly powers (79b). Similarly the intercessions from the Eucharistic Prayer invoke the saints. As well, they are made on earth for the living and for those dead in waiting for the fullness of life in Christ with the saints (79g). The connection with the saints is retained in the maintenance of the custom of placing the relics of a martyr under an altar that is about to be dedicated (302). The relics must be authentic and can be of a saint who is not a martyr. Yet the preference for those of a martyr reflects early Christian beliefs in the power of their intercession and the galvanizing effects of the stories of their deaths.

THE CHURCH AS PILGRIM

The church as pilgrim complements the earlier image of the church as holy. If holiness comes from Christ, the pilgrim church is concerned with the sanctification of life, purification and ongoing reform in light of sin, and responding to changed conditions in human society.

The sanctification of the moments of human life is linked to the grace of the paschal mystery. This is laid out in a paragraph based on the Constitution of the Sacred Liturgy (SC 61):

> Since the liturgy of the Sacraments and Sacramentals causes, for the faithful who are properly disposed, almost every event in life to be sanctified by divine grace that flows from the paschal mystery, and because the Eucharist is the Sacrament of Sacraments, the Missal provides formularies for Masses and orations that may be used in the various circumstances of Christian life, for the needs

of the whole world or for the needs of the Church, whether universal or local. (368)

The principle of sanctification is reflected in the pastoral nature of the *General Instruction.* The Missal contains an array of options precisely so that the liturgy as celebrated can correspond to the needs, spiritual preparation, and capacity of the participants (352).

At the same time, any celebration of the liturgy itself offers a challenge of ongoing conversion to the participants: *Though holy in its origin, this people nevertheless grows continually in holiness by its conscious, active, and fruitful participation in the mystery of the Eucharist* (5). To this effect the offering in the Eucharistic Prayer is considered an act of self-offering, which leads to the divinization of all things in God:

> *The Church's intention, however, is that the faithful not only offer this spotless Victim but also learn to offer themselves, and so day by day to be consummated, through Christ the Mediator, into unity with God and with each other, so that at last God may be all in all.* (79f)

The high point of unity, both with God and with one another, is the reception of Holy Communion: *it is a people made one by sharing in the Communion of Christ's Body and Blood* (5).

As well, the *General Instruction* contains some admonitions, directed here at the lay faithful, which serve to remind us that at worship we can be only too human. The *Instruction* calls the faithful to love of neighbor: *They should, moreover, endeavour to make this clear by their deep religious sense and their charity toward brothers and sisters who participate with them in the same celebration* (95). The same paragraph invites the lay baptized to set aside any division or individualism since all are children of the one Father: *Thus they are to shun any appearance of individualism or division, keeping before their eyes that they have only one Father in heaven and accordingly are all brothers and sisters to each other.* The rite of peace is understood as a sign of unity and charity (82). As for individualism and favoritism, any custom of reserving seats for private persons is to be abolished and never revived (311). The Lord's Prayer is associated with the purification from sin (81), while the act of penitence (51) is a reminder of the fallibility of the members of the church.

Conversion and sanctification require attention to the concrete circumstances of the people at prayer. They take place within and through culture, place, history, and language. This is reflected throughout the *General Instruction,* however, much of it can be seen in paragraph 15. There we find a rationale for the new things brought forth in the Missal. Some ancient expressions have been accommodated to contemporary needs and circumstances. Others have been modified to bring them into line with the new state of the present world, the language of modern theology, and the actual state of current church discipline. As well, the changed state of the world has led to new compositions, often drawing on the language of recent conciliar documents. The *Instruction* acknowledges that this "broader" view is in fact part of the very nature of the church and seeks further understanding of this dynamic: *but also an understanding and a more profound study of the Church's entire past and of all the ways in which her one and only faith has been set forth in the quite diverse human and social forms prevailing in Semitic, Greek, and Latin areas* (9).

THE CHURCH AND THE POOR

The church at worship holds the poor and the needy with special regard. This is reflected in the *General Instruction* in a number of places. The most explicit mention of the poor is with regard to the preparation of the gifts: *It is well also that money or other gifts for the poor or for the Church, brought by the faithful or collected in the church, should be received. These are to be put in a suitable place but away from the Eucharistic table* (73). From this we can see that concern for the poor should have a place in the liturgy, as well as in the minds and hearts of those who make up the celebration. The gifts for the poor are in relationship with the gifts of bread and wine and any gifts to the church. There is a simple idea at play here. It is God who feeds us from the eucharistic table, with gifts that the divine goodness provided in the first place. As we are fed so freely from God's bounty are we not then obliged to feed others? After all, it is ultimately God's largess. The same goes for what the church acquires. The eucharistic imperative to attend to the poor is evident in the provision that gifts for the poor be part of the procession of the bread and the wine during the Holy Thursday evening Mass of the Lord's Supper.

Active participation in the mystery of the Eucharist, itself an act of ongoing conversion, should also lead to action on behalf of the needy. When dealing with the rites of dismissal, the *General Instruction* sets together praise of God and good works. Just as the act of thanksgiving to God ought to make us a eucharistic people, so the great works of God ought to lead us to do the works of God. The GIRM reads: *The concluding rites consist of* [among other things]...*the dismissal of the people by the deacon or the priest, so that each may go out to do good works, praising and blessing God* (90c). The dynamic reflects that found in the first two chapters of the Letter to the Ephesians, and in particular Ephesians 2:10: *For we are what he has made us, created in Christ Jesus for good works, which God prepared beforehand to be our way of life.*

The Priestly Nature of the Church

Yet, in the *General Instruction* care for the poor and needy goes beyond charity and good works. The people of

God at Eucharist prays for the needs of the world: *It is a people called to bring to God the prayers of the entire human family* (5). This is a priestly role. The Letter to the Hebrews speaks of the priest as the one who comes from the people but offers prayers and sacrifices on their behalf (Heb 5:1). The church in Christ takes up this role on behalf of the salvation of all (69), for the needs of the whole world (368), and for those burdened under any kind of difficulty in particular (70). These paragraphs are devoted to the General Intercessions (69, 70), and to Masses and prayers for various circumstances (368). The church is priestly because its prayers are made in and through Christ, the one mediator. Perhaps the church is at its most priestly when it prays for those who are so lost and forgotten that they have no one to pray for them. Such a church truly reflects the mystery of God's redemptive love and the priestly intercession of Christ.

THE CHURCH AS HIERARCHICAL

The most prominent understanding of the church throughout the *General Instruction* is that of the church arrayed hierarchically. This is both a little surprising and quite understandable. The Dogmatic Constitution on the Church from Vatican II deals with the hierarchical nature of the church only after a chapter each on the Church as Mystery and as the People of God. The *Instruction* is not so careful. Yet it is primarily a practical document, and questions of order, function, role, and rights are continual concerns. We are left to ask what is the understanding of hierarchy being put forward and how congruent is this with the other images of church present in the *Instruction*.

It is important to distinguish between a theology of hierarchy and a theology of priesthood. They are inextricably interwoven throughout the *Instruction,* where in fact we meet discussion of priesthood, ministerial (4) and baptized (5), before we are introduced to the hierarchical order.

Nevertheless, a separate discussion of hierarchy allows us to concentrate on the "order" of the church, while priesthood is more a question of the ministries within that order. Consequently, we are able to ask more clearly about the nature of hierarchy as understood by the GIRM, and to avoid the pitfall of reducing hierarchy to those ordained bishop and priest. There is a second pitfall that is worth naming ahead of time. Our recurrent experience leads us to identify hierarchical order with the petty tyranny too often imposed by the clergy on worshipers. Instances include statements that begin: *the bishop wants..., or Father says we must do it this way....* Hierarchy as a system is not about the arbitrary imposition of the will of an absolutist ruler. That is more akin to despotism. Rather, it is about the rights and responsibilities of all members across the various levels within a system. With regard to this the idea of the church as hierarchy is about even more. It involves an understanding of hierarchical ordering that gives not just stable government but manifests both the church in Christ and the face of Christ to the world. The *Instruction* is attentive to this point. Is hierarchy the best form of ordering for the contemporary church? That question is important but is outside the scope of our present study. Nor can it be answered unless there is a clearer understanding of what hierarchy implies for liturgy.

The hierarchical ordering of the eucharistic celebration is clearly stated in four places: 16ff., 91, 112, 294. The content of these paragraphs is given further emphasis because of their placement in the *Instruction*. Paragraphs 16, 91, and 112 open respectively chapter I on the importance and dignity of the eucharistic celebration, chapter III on the duties and ministries in the Mass, and chapter IV on the different forms of celebrating Mass. Paragraph 294 is part of the section setting out the general principles for the arrangement and furnishing of churches (chapter V). Hierarchy, then, is a guiding principle for each of these aspects of the celebration of the Mass. We will base our comments on paragraph 91:

*The Eucharistic celebration is an action of Christ
and the Church, namely, the holy people united and
ordered under the Bishop. It therefore pertains to
the whole Body of the Church, manifests it, and has
its effect upon it. It also affects the individual members of the Church in different ways, according to
their different orders, offices, and actual participation. In this way, the Christian people, "a chosen
race, a royal priesthood, a holy nation, God's own
people," expresses its cohesion and its hierarchical
ordering. All, therefore, whether they are ordained
ministers or lay Christian faithful, in fulfilling their
office or their duty, should carry out solely but
completely that which pertains to them.* (91)

The paragraph opens up a number of key understandings. First among them is that any hierarchical manifestation in worship is in light of and accountable to the action
of Christ in the church. The role of Christ and his presence
in the church as his body ought to direct our theology and
practice of hierarchy.

A second point is that in the *Instruction* the preeminent expression of the body of Christ as a hierarchy is
found in that liturgy under the diocesan bishop. This especially is related to occasions when the bishop presides, sur-
rounded by the presbyterate, deacons, and lay ministers,
with the faithful actively and fully participating (112).
Consequently, the *Instruction* makes it clear that every
legitimate celebration of the Eucharist is directed by the
bishop personally or through the priests as his helpers (92).

Our third point now becomes evident. The diocesan
bishop is the highest of a number of hierarchical levels.
These include the presbyters, the deacons, and the lay
faithful. The hierarchical nature of the church is most manifest when all levels are operative together, with all members carrying out the respective duties of their orders and
offices. These points are underscored throughout the document. The centrality of the local bishop, as opposed to any

member of the Episcopal rank, is seen in the rubrics for the Eucharistic Prayer. They state that, aside from the bishop of Rome, only the diocesan bishop, coadjutor, and auxiliary bishops are to be named. Other bishops who happen to be present are not named (149). The differentiation of duties is seen in the care that the GIRM takes to distinguish between the role of presiding and that of proclaiming the Gospel. That function falls to the deacon, or at least a con-celebrant, and only as a last resort to a presider (59). Under the *Instruction* members of one level cannot simply usurp roles that are not theirs. This is applied to the office of reader: *In the Eucharistic Celebration, the lector has his own proper office, which he must exercise personally* (99).

This leads us to a fourth point. The cohesion of the liturgical assembly is not guaranteed by hierarchical struc-tures in themselves. A celebration is cohesive when the practice respects the differentiation of tasks, and allows for active and full participation by all who have gathered. For the faithful, participation is a right and a duty they have from baptism (19). This implies both that the bishop will ensure their rights and that the laity will gladly serve (97). Anything less that this form of participation negatively impacts on all members of the assembly, chafes at the cohesion of the body, and reduces the ecclesial nature of the celebration.

What is it, then, that makes up the different levels within the hierarchical church? The GIRM does not directly address this question, but leaves some markers. The ordained members of the hierarchical church are not given more dignity than the lay members. Consequently, during the preparation of the gifts bishop, priest, and people may be incensed (75), with the thurible swung back and forth the same number of times (three) for each (277). Rather, the focus in the GIRM falls to the different min-istries and actions: *The People of God, gathered for Mass, has a coherent and hierarchical structure, which finds its expression in the variety of ministries and the variety of actions according to the different parts of the celebration*

(294). The diversity of vestments is said to symbolize office, not dignity: *This variety of offices in the celebration of the Eucharist is shown outwardly by the diversity of sacred vestments, which should therefore be a sign of the office proper to each minister* (335). There is a focus too on service, with bishops and priests reminded that they are servants of the liturgy (24) and are to serve the spiritual good of the people (352).

Yet it would be unwise to assume that those who have been given more important hierarchical status are immune from the deficiencies of such a structure. At one point the *Instruction* collapses the church into the ordained:

> *Even if it is sometimes not possible to have the presence and active participation of the faithful, which bring out more plainly the ecclesial nature of the celebration, the Eucharistic Celebration always retains its efficacy and dignity because it is the action of Christ and the Church, in which the priest fulfils his own principal office and always acts for the people's salvation.* (19)

The *Instruction,* then, is most attentive to the theology of hierarchy. This reflects its practical nature. It seeks a hierarchy of ministry, not of dignity, across all the members of the assembly. As such, it reflects the diversity of roles, and is properly enacted when there is full, conscious, and active participation.

SUMMARY

There is no single theology of church in the GIRM. The predominance of a theology of hierarchy warrants close attention to what is actually meant by the term. It is not another word for despotism or tyranny. Interwoven throughout the *Instruction* are allusions to the church as bride, as holy people of God, as body of Christ, and as the community of the baptized. These biblical references are set alongside the church as apostolic and as foretaste of the reign of God. Ultimately there is no attempt at a systematic theology of church, and it remains to be seen how effectively the various theological currents converge and modify one another. However, the church as mystery does not stop at theological considerations alone, but requires attention to its structures. Of course, they are not without theological underpinnings themselves.

THE STRUCTURE OF THE CHURCH

Any discussion of the theology of the church needs to be complemented with a review of how the *General Instruction* understands the actual historical reality of the current church. Here we meet an interconnected range of structures. We have noted above the emphasis on the particular church, the diocese under its bishop. Related to this is the regional Conference of Bishops, and indeed groupings of Conferences with a common language. Yet we are dealing with an *Institutio* for the Missal of the Roman Church, itself under the reform mandate of the Second Vatican Council. The *Instruction* acknowledges also that the body of Christ is broader than the Roman tradition.

It is worth recalling here that each celebration of the Eucharist is understood as the act of a unique gathering of the community, which manifests the church itself, especially the Sunday parish Eucharist: *Great importance should also be attached to a Mass celebrated with any community, but especially with the parish community, inasmuch as it represents the universal Church gathered at a given time and place. This is particularly true in the communal Sunday celebration* (113). Another way each celebration is said to give presence to the universal church is seen through the description of the priest at Mass as one who prays in the name of both the church and the community gathered (33). From these individual celebrations we can move to the structure within which they are prayed.

THE PARTICULAR CHURCH

The *Instruction* assigns the utmost importance to the celebration of the Eucharist in a particular church. It especially gives value to the Mass celebrated by the diocesan bishop in which the presbyterate, deacons, and lay faithful participate (22). The ordering of the Mass, as an act of Christ and his church, falls to the bishop (91). Each celebration, then, is seen to fall within a diocese and under its episcopal oversight. We will take up this oversight in detail in the section specifically on the liturgical ministry of the bishop.

The GIRM also speaks of Conferences of Bishops and indeed of groupings of Conferences. Conferences have the power to place before the Apostolic See for approval decisions on a series of adaptations to the *Instruction* and the Order of the Mass (390). They have responsibility for the vernacular translation of Latin texts (392) and the musical forms, melodies, and instruments for worship (393). Single Conferences, or a combination of Conferences, can undertake the drawing up of a proper national or territorial calendar (394). Wherever possible, the *Instruction* sets out that regions with common language should use the same translations (392). Each individual diocese, then, is understood in collaboration with the other dioceses with its Conference, region, and language group.

THE APOSTOLIC SEE

The task of collegial unity in worship is situated within the offices of the Apostolic See, itself the curial arm of the bishop of Rome. The *Instruction* sets out the following principle: *Furthermore the principle shall be respected according to which each particular Church must be in accord with the universal Church not only regarding the doctrine of the faith and sacramental signs, but also to usages universally handed down by apostolic and unbroken tradition* (397). The promulgation of the typical editions of rites falls to the bishop of Rome, and, consequently, the Roman Missal and this *General Instruction* are the work of the Apostolic See. Any adaptation that a Conference of Bishops wishes to make requires the recognition of the Apostolic See (397).

In practice the relationship among the particular churches, the Conferences, and the Apostolic See, as set out in its *General Instruction,* has some tensions. The *Instruction* necessarily deals with the Roman Rite and rightly guards its traditions and theology. However, it seems unnecessary, and too defensive, to raise and summarily dismiss the question of other families of rites for the worldwide, culturally and linguistically diverse, Roman Church (398). More importantly there are questions about the recognition by the Apostolic See of adaptations requested by a Conference. No list of criteria is provided for the granting or refusal of a *recognitio*. Some can be gleaned from the *Instruction* itself: unity of doctrine, of sacramental signs, of apostolic usage, of traditional usage; the maintenance of notable and precious parts of the Roman liturgical heritage; the identity and unitary expression of the Roman Rite (397); genuine and definite benefit to the church; organic development from existing forms; a cautious and unhurried change (398); and the maintenance of a certain variety of customs (399). These points are open to a degree of scholarly debate and subjective interpretation. It can be asked whether all the areas of possible adaptation listed in paragraph 390 are central to unity of doctrine, tradition, and identity. There also seems to be something of a shift in the meaning given to the recognition. Its original sense was that the work presented by a Conference of Bishops and conformed to the needs of the particular churches was recognized as within the Roman tradition. Since the late 1990s, the emphasis appears to have fallen on Bishops' Conferences producing the type of text that the curia will approve.

THE CHURCH IN ECUMENICAL COUNCIL

The *Instruction* itself falls under the reforms of the Second Vatican Council. Both the first paragraph of the GIRM and the penultimate (398) refer to the norms of the Council. In that sense the pope and his curia, the Conferences of Bishops, and diocesan bishops are all challenged to implement those principles and decisions from the Council, and issued by the bishop of Rome in union with the bishops of the particular churches within the Roman Church. The church in ecumenical council is the ecclesial structural principle upon which the *Instruction* is based.

THE CHURCH UNIVERSAL

While not the major concern of the GIRM, there are references to aspects of the universal church. The insistence on the integrity and value of the Roman Rite is itself a reminder that there are other rites within the Roman umbrella (SC 4) and beyond it, especially in the particular churches of the East (397). We have here a practical demonstration that the *Instruction* falls under the broad cloak of the universal body of Christ as one, holy, catholic, and apostolic.

THE CHURCH AS A BUILDING

For many, many people the church is not primarily a theological or social reality; rather, it is a building. This is but one of the many occasions in liturgy where our language shows its limits. The problem is in both Latin and English. The *Instruction* deals with this in the first paragraph of chapter V on the arrangement and furnishings of churches. It immediately distinguishes between the church as the people of God and the building in which they gather, the church. The building is secondary. The celebration of the Eucharist is primary: *For the celebration of the Eucharist, the people of God normally are gathered together in a church or, if there is no church or if it is too small, then in another respectable place that is nonetheless worthy of so great a mystery* (288). History and pastoral necessity have shown us the variety of places that have fallen under the term *respectable*. The mystery is not revealed in or by the building. In the first place it is revealed by the celebration itself of the people of God. That is not to say that the building is of no great importance. They should be worthy, beautiful, heavenward (288), contemporary yet traditional, nourishing of faith and devotion, and suitable for the rites (289). The *Instruction* reminds us, however, that our language can be a little deceptive. Our churches are at the service of the people of God, who make up the church.

CONCLUSION

The governing ecclesial concerns of the *General Instruction* are the church as a hierarchical organization, and the Roman liturgy enacted in particular churches under the auspices of the bishop of Rome in light of the Second Vatican Council. Throughout the document are other reflections on church: scriptural, apostolic, pastoral and missionary, ecumenical and eschatological. They provide much of the rich texture of the GIRM and allow for a deeper theological appreciation of the liturgy. Ultimately these secondary understandings provide the deepest sense of the church at worship, offer a critique of the *Instruction* itself, and give word and image to the mystery of the church.

CHAPTER FOUR

THE PEOPLE OF GOD ARRAYED HIERARCHICALLY

> *The Bishop should therefore be determined that the priests, the deacons, and the lay Christian faithful grasp ever more deeply the genuine meaning of the rites and liturgical texts, and thereby be led to an active and fruitful celebration of the Eucharist.* (22)

The *General Instruction* teaches that the people of God is arrayed hierarchically when it celebrates the Eucharist. All the members of the church are allocated a place in this order, which secures their rights and sets out their obligations. Building on our discussions in the previous chapter, we are in a position to examine how hierarchy is expressed in the rites and texts of the celebration.

THE DIOCESAN BISHOP

The *General Instruction,* following the Constitution on the Sacred Liturgy (41, 42), sets the diocesan bishop at the center of the celebration of the renewed liturgy. This is shown to best effect in two paragraphs inserted into the third edition of the *Instruction,* 22 and 387. They offer a compelling vision for his leadership and oversight. The diocesan bishop is described, in a somewhat mixed metaphor, as the high priest of his flock (387). He is regarded as a key focal point of the lives in Christ of the members of this flock (387) and the chief steward of the mysteries of God for the diocese (22). There is a close relationship drawn here between the pastoral life of the faithful and their worship. The bishop is seen as the moderator, promoter, and guardian of the liturgical life of the particular church (22). The same set of ideas is expressed in another way: *[the diocesan bishop] must promote, regulate, and be vigilant over the liturgical life in his diocese* (387). This is not simply about rubrics, oversight, and exerting control; it is first and foremost about developing in all the baptized an authentic liturgical spirituality and a love for worship so that priests, deacons, and laity alike may always grasp a genuine sense of the rites and liturgical celebrations (22). The *Institutio* makes this even clearer when it says: *With him lies responsibility above all for fostering the spirit of the sacred Liturgy in the priests, deacons, and faithful* (387). We have here an important restating of that often forgotten principle in the Constitution on the Sacred Liturgy that urges pastors of souls to realize that in the celebration of the liturgy something more is required than the laws governing valid and lawful celebration (SC 11). The first duty of the diocesan bishop, then, is to foster the spirit of the liturgy.

Because the bishop is the chief steward of the worship in a particular church, the celebrations at which he presides are given great importance. They are understood to manifest the mystery of the church (22), to give expression to the unity of the church across its hierarchical ordering (91), and to reveal something of the mystery of the church as the sacrament of unity (92). Accordingly, the concelebration of the priests of the diocese with the bishop is given strong encouragement, particularly at the more solemn feasts of the liturgical year and at important diocesan celebrations (199, 203).

Celebrations led by the bishop should also serve as examples to the diocese of the spirit of the liturgy in practice, incorporating a genuine sense of the rites, of the active and fruitful celebration, and of the beauty of place, music, and art (22). As well, there are particular roles and honors ascribed to the bishop, whether he is presiding or has assigned that role to another (92, 112, 117, 149, 175, 212).

The *General Instruction* sets out both the norms that the local bishop can establish and the ones that he falls under. The bishop is responsible for regulating concelebration, the ministry of service to the priest at the altar, Communion under both kinds, the construction and arrangement of churches (387), and the local calendar (394). He can give permission for the celebration across the diocese of a Mass suited to a serious need or pastoral situation (374). He also takes part in the decisions made by the Conference of Bishops (388–96).

His governance is understood to fall within the liturgy and not over it (24). According to the *General Instruction,* he presides in light of the norms in the Ceremonial of Bishops (112). The *Instruction's* chapter on architecture relates the bishop's moderation of church buildings and their furnishings to a Diocesan Commission on the Sacred Liturgy and Art. It does so in two ways. The first establishes the commission as the central consultative body for any church construction, restoration, and remodeling. The second requires the bishop too to seek its counsel: *The diocesan Bishop, moreover, should use the counsel and help of this commission whenever it comes to laying down norms on this matter, approving plans for new buildings, and making decisions on the more important issues* (291). This would include advice on the placement of the tabernacle (315). Both points have been taken from the Constitution on the Sacred Liturgy (45, 126). Ultimately the *Instruction* calls on the bishops to make decisions for the pastoral and spiritual well-being of their flock, rather than from personal preference:

> ...the utmost care must be taken to choose and to
> arrange those forms and elements set forth by the

Church that, in view of the circumstances of the people and the place, will more effectively foster active and full participation and more properly respond to the spiritual needs of the faithful. (20)

An important challenge is left to us. How can the wider church—liturgical experts, clergy, and lay faithful—help the bishop to understand the norms of the GIRM, empower an appropriate liturgical commission or its equivalent, assess pastoral needs, and infuse in the diocese the spirit of the liturgy?

THE *SACERDOS:* BISHOP AND PRIEST TOGETHER

Any discussion of the priest in the liturgy has to deal with a shortcoming in our English-language liturgical vocabulary. Often the *General Instruction* uses the term *sacerdos*. Strictly speaking, it means more than the English word *priest,* its usual and most appropriate translation. It refers to anyone who has attained the office of presbyter, in effect, signaling both bishops and priests. When the *Instruction* needs to make some distinction between these two ranks of the *sacerdotes* the Latin utilizes the term *presbyter* for the minister we generally call the priest. Here we will follow the custom of our language while remaining mindful that priest connotes bishops and the members of the presbyterium.

Perhaps it is best to be somewhat blunt when examining the various currents that are brought together in the *Instruction* around the theology of priesthood. The GIRM contains two different theologies of priesthood. Some features overlap, and at the surface there appears to be harmony. Their differences, however, are a cause of continuing tension. To a large extent the *Instruction* has retrieved the ancient patristic heritage of the bishop, and by extension the priest, as the pastoral leader of the community and the one who rightly presides at the communal Eucharist. Here, the focus falls on the unity of presider and assembly, the manifestation of the church, and the fullest celebration of the mystery—an approach that gives great attention to the best possible celebration of the Sunday Eucharist. Under this theology, when the bishop or priest prays in the name of the people, he is understood as the authentic leader who guides and gathers their prayer, enabling the liturgy to be an act of the very church itself. Emphasis here falls first on the bishop as the center of unity, and then on the priest as one who can stand in the place of the bishop.

At the same time, the GIRM has retained from medieval and tridentine usage a theology that expresses that the priest acts in the liturgy in the "person" of Christ. Here the emphasis falls on the efficacy of the eucharistic sacrifice, guaranteed by the validity of the ordination of the minister and his obedient enactment of the rite. Consequently, the distinction between the Sunday celebration and any other celebration is considerably weakened. Another effect is that the role of presiding over an assembly becomes secondary to ritual performance. Thus, the participation of the assembly is seen as of lesser importance, and, in some cases, negated. Emphasis in this case falls on the priest as an ordained minister.

The *Institutio* sets both theologies side by side on a number of occasions (30, 93). The earliest is as follows:

> *Further, the nature of the ministerial priesthood proper to a Bishop and a priest [presbyter], who offer the Sacrifice in the person of Christ and who preside over the gathering of the holy people, is evident in the form of the rite itself, by reason of the more prominent place and office of the priest [sacerdos].* (4)

This paragraph is most interesting. It sets offering sacrifice and presiding together, as expected. It relates to both bishop and priest *(presbyter)* as priests *(sacerdotes)*. As well, in offering the form of the rite as an argument, it also provides that same form as an avenue of critique. Like the *Instruction,* we can ask how well the form of the rites supports either of these theologies of ordained ministry. We will now turn to a more detailed examination of the *General Instruction,* first for what it says about the priest in the person of Christ, and then about the priest as president of the assembly.

THE PRIEST "IN THE PERSON OF CHRIST"

The *Instruction* is actually quite circumspect about the priest as acting in the person of Christ. It is related most directly to the presidential prayers—the Eucharistic Prayer, the collect, the prayer over the offerings, and the prayer after Communion: *These prayers are addressed to God in the name of the entire holy people and all present, by the priest who presides over the assembly in the person of Christ. It is with good reason, therefore, that they are called the "presidential prayers"* (30). Just because they are said to be prayers in the person of Christ does not imply that they can be said in any slipshod fashion: *The nature of the "presidential" texts demands that they be spoken in a loud and clear voice and that everyone listen with attention* (32). Throughout the *Instruction* there appear to be no other roles of the presider that are considered as in the person of Christ. Three questions can be raised. What are the implications in the *General Instruction* from this? What interpretations of "in the person of Christ" are read into the GIRM? How well do the ritual forms support this theology?

On two occasions the *Instruction* makes allowance for the Mass to be celebrated without any other person or minister present than the priest himself. The first occurs early in the discussion of the importance and dignity of the eucharistic celebration. It maintains that when the presence and participation of the people is not possible the priest suffices. The basis for this is that the office of priest encompasses the action of Christ, the action of the church, and the priestly action on behalf of the people's salvation (19). A second number prohibits the celebration of Mass without at least one minister except for a just and reasonable cause (254). The prior edition of the GIRM was stronger than this (1975 GIRM 211), but the modification reflects the later 1983 Code of Canon Law (CIC 906). There is a reaffirmation of the actual communal nature of the celebration with the denial of permission to celebrate individually either the Mass of the Lord's Supper or the Easter Vigil (199). These two numbers pose an unfortunate theological and psychological dilemma for the priests and for the deacons and people alike. Are the functions of the deacon and those of the people essential to the celebration of the liturgy? If not, what does it mean to preside, to respect and foster their ministries, and to elicit their responses? The way is open for the priest to presume that the Mass is "his" and that he privately embodies both Christ and the church. This would be an extreme interpretation of the teaching that one of the modes of Christ's presence in the liturgy is in the person of the minister (27).

While the *General Instruction* itself is very restrained, other ecclesial writings contain a much more expansive theology and spirituality of the priest precisely *in persona Christi*. This makes it very difficult to avoid reading the *Institutio* in light of broader interpretations, which may in fact be foreign to the restraint of our liturgical document.

How well do the presidential prayers express such a theology? There are a number of questions here. The interpretation in the GIRM of the collect prayer runs somewhat counter to the original patristic understanding. Currently the emphasis falls on the prayer of the priest, understood as a priestly prayer of petition, which mediates the petition, praise, and homage of the assembly. The Amen of the people serves to unite them to the more central priestly prayer. The ancient understanding was, however, that the priest's oration both gathered the petitions of the faithful, made during the silence, and gathered the assembly into a single unit. The people's Amen ratified and confirmed the presiding celebrant's prayer. Originally the emphasis fell on the petitions of the faithful and their Amen, which were served by the presidential prayer.[1]

By tradition, the Eucharistic Prayer has been known as the *priestly prayer* and is the preeminent prayer in the Mass. This, however, has been taken to mean that only the priest prays the prayer. The GIRM reflects something of this: *The Eucharistic Prayer demands, by its very nature, that only the priest say it in virtue of his ordination* (147). This statement, if taken in isolation, is not quite accurate. Eucharistic Prayers, by their nature, contained and still contain parts for priest and for the assembly. In the Eastern tradition some prayers contain parts for the deacon as well. This is also reflected in the *Instruction,* which prescribes not only silence and reverent attention while the presiding celebrant proclaims his parts but also participation by the people, deacon, and concelebrants in the dialogue, the Holy, Holy, Holy, the acclamation, and the great Amen: *The people, for their part, should associate themselves with the priest in faith and in silence, as well as through their parts as prescribed in the course of the Eucharistic Prayer* (147). According to the *Institutio's* description of the doxology, it is the people's Amen that actually concludes the prayer: *Final doxology: By which the glorification of God is expressed and which is confirmed and concluded by the people's acclamation, Amen* (79h). The participation of the people, then, is an integral part of the prayer itself. This is reinforced by the seriousness with which the *General Instruction* treats the dialogues in the Mass, including the Preface dialogue (34, 35).

There is a second qualification to the sense of the prayer as a priestly prayer. From the texts themselves, ancient and contemporary, the priest does not pray in his own name. Rather he prays in the name of the gathered assembly. This accounts for the continual use of the first person plural *we* throughout the prayers. Across the centuries the very rare exceptions to this usually refer to additions used when the priest is celebrating his anniversary of ordination.

In some circles much emphasis has been laid on the recitation by the priest of the words of Christ during the institution narrative and consecration. The *Instruction* offers some caution. This part of the prayer is held in high esteem, and can be accompanied by genuflections (43), kneeling or bowing (43, 179), incense and bells (150). There is provision for the priest celebrant to bow while reciting the words of the Lord (275c). This is immediately followed by an acclamation of the mystery of faith (151). At a concelebration the GIRM instructs that all concelebrants speak the words of consecration (218). As well, it sensibly retains the solution to the dilemma of the celebrant discovering that the liquid in the chalice is not wine: he repeats over a wine-filled chalice the part of the institution narrative related to the cup (324). At the same time, the *Instruction* names this part of the prayer in two ways, as institution narrative and consecration (79d). By doing so it calls attention to its place in the prayer as one element in an extended and integrated oration. The Eucharistic Prayer, then, is not presented as a consecration formula with a long but less important prelude and postlude.

This cautious approach is justified by two further points. First, the words of the institution narrative are not a direct scriptural quotation. They are rather a liturgical interpretation of the various Last Supper blessing narratives in the three Synoptic Gospels and St. Paul.[2] They are undoubtedly based in the scripture, but they cannot be seen as a literal rendition of the scripture, less so as direct words of Jesus himself. Second, contemporary scholarship has contributed further to our understanding of the eucharistic theology of the first seven centuries of the church's life, a fact that the *Instruction* takes into account (7, 8, 9). The permission from the Church of Rome for admission to the Eucharist between the Chaldean Church and the Assyrian Church of the East centers on the recognition of the validity of the ancient Eucharistic Prayer known as the Anaphora of Addai and Mari.[3] This prayer does not contain the Last Supper institution narrative, nor the words of consecration. The recognition of the validity of this prayer forces us to broaden our theology of consecration beyond that contained in the *Instruction* (3, 218).

The *General Instruction* contains a theology of the priest as acting in the person of Christ that offers an interpretation of the way the Mass is an action of Christ, along with a form of guarantee of validity and efficacy. The use of this theology allows for the continuance of practices such as a priest celebrating Mass with no one else receiving Communion, or indeed, with no one else present. Yet any overidentification of the priest with Christ can compromise the participation of all other ministers and faithful present. Nor does it sit so comfortably with the nature of the collect-style prayers or the Eucharistic Prayer.

THE PRIEST AS "PRESIDER"

The second theology of priesthood in the GIRM is built on a theology of the priest as president of the assembly. As presider, the priest directs the celebration of the Eucharist (92). His role is described as follows:

> *A priest also, who possesses within the Church the power of Holy Order to offer sacrifice in the person of Christ, stands for this reason at the head of the faithful people gathered together here and now, presides over their prayer, proclaims the message of salvation to them, associates the people with himself in the offering of sacrifice through Christ in the Holy Spirit to God the Father, gives his brothers and sisters the Bread of eternal life, and partakes of it with them. (93)*

He is the primary minister of the celebration. He is not the only minister, but the celebration cannot take place without him. Like all ministers in the liturgy, he is constrained to do all those parts, but only those parts, that belong to his office (91).

A significant amount of the *Instruction* is taken up with elucidating the role of the presider. The GIRM is very clear that presiding is a single role of authentic leadership amid the gathered assembly. This should not be compromised in any way: *One and the same priest celebrant must always exercise the presidential office in all of its parts, except for those parts which are proper to a Mass at which the Bishop is present* (108).

This presidency is carried out in a number of ways. There are rites and prayers that the presider leads, such as the liturgy of the word, the final blessing (31), the sign of the cross which opens the liturgy (50), the collect-style prayers (54), the preparation of the gifts (75), and the Eucharistic Prayer (78). The *General Instruction* gives particular value to the dialogues: *in fact, they are not simply outward signs of communal celebration but foster and bring about communion between priest and people* (34). There are parts of the Mass, such as the Gloria (53) and the Creed (68), that presider and people enact in unison. The most significant of these, perhaps, is listening to the word of God. According to the *General Instruction,* the proclamation of the word is a ministerial function, not presidential (59). The readings fall to a lay reader, while the Gospel is read by the deacon or, in his absence, a concelebrant (59). The presiding celebrant only reads the Gospel by default. The message of the liturgy is clear: all fall under the scriptures, bishop, priest, and people alike. There are parts of the rite that the presider may either take up himself or allow another to assume, including direction giving (43), the brief introduction to the Mass of the day (50), the homily (66), and the breaking of the bread at Communion (83). There are occasions when the presider can offer introductory comments and instructions: at the beginning of Mass, before the readings, before the Eucharistic Prayer, and before the dismissal (31). The *Institutio* commands brevity.

Finally, there are prayers that the presider says alone and inaudibly. These are the private prayers through which the celebrant seeks divine assistance to exercise his ministry attentively and devotedly (33).

The *General Instruction* recognizes that presiders require skills to preside. The eucharistic celebration should be carried out with a sense of great reverence and adoration (3). The "presidential" prayers need to be spoken loudly, clearly, and so that the faithful listen with attention (32). In declaiming texts the presider ought to be aware of their genre and should offer them in a tone suited to the form of celebration and solemnity of the gathering, and in tune with the idiom and culture of the people (38). Adaptations and remarks should be done succinctly and in accordance with the sense of the Missal (31). The ability to sing is a bonus (147). The *Instruction* does not, however, reduce these requirements in the presider to skills alone. They involve an underlying attitude of service and humility: *When he celebrates the Eucharist, therefore, he must serve God and the people with dignity and humility, and by his bearing and by the way he says the divine words he must convey to the faithful the living presence of God* (93). Presiding at the Eucharist involves the whole person of the presider. The importance of this is highlighted by its application in the Directory for Masses with Children:

> *It is the responsibility of the priest who celebrates with children to make the celebration festive, familial, and meditative. Even more than in Masses with adults, the priest is the one to create this kind of attitude, which depends on his personal preparation and his manner of acting and speaking with others.* (DMC 23)

Ascribing a role to the personality and style of the priest predates the Vatican II reform of the liturgy. During the debates at the Council of Trent concerning aspects of the efficacy of the Mass, a number of theologians gave prominence to the devotion and intention of the priest as he performed the liturgy.[4] The central point is that the nature of presiding itself demands that the person and personality of the celebrant play a role. However, he is at work in service of the liturgy, not over it.

There are many choices to be made in the celebration of the Mass in the Roman Rite. Oversight of the celebration falls to the priest so that there is harmonious and diligent planning by all concerned. It demands respect for the rites and their musical parts. It is to be pastorally appropriate. Furthermore, it is said to involve consultation:

> *Among all who are involved with regard to the rites, pastoral aspects, and music there should be harmony and diligence in the effective preparation of each liturgical celebration in accord with the Missal and other liturgical books. This should take place under the direction of the rector of the church and after the consultation with the faithful about things that directly pertain to them. The priest who presides at the celebration, however, always retains the right of arranging those things that are his own responsibility.* (111)

Even here the criteria by which he makes choices do not fall to him. Rather they are given in the *Instruction*. The paragraph above has introduced the criterion of attentiveness to the genre of the prayer or rite. Other examples of this are the provision that the deacon exercise his ministry when present at the eucharistic celebration (171) and that on solemnities a priest follow the calendar of the diocese where he is celebrating (353). The provision for the use of extraordinary ministers of Holy Communion is based in respect for the rites by not overly and unnecessarily prolonging them (162).

There is a clear statement of the criteria for making choices at the beginning of chapter VII. These are based around the principles of pastoral effectiveness, the common spiritual good of the people, appropriate consultation, and thorough planning. The very reason for the presence of choices in the first place is the pastoral effectiveness of the church's worship. The paragraphs read:

> *The pastoral effectiveness of a celebration will be greatly increased if the texts of the readings, the prayers, and the liturgical songs correspond as closely as possible to the needs, spiritual prepara-tion, and culture of those taking part. This is achieved by appropriate use of the wide options described below.*
>
> *The priest, therefore, in planning the celebra-tion of Mass, should have in mind the common spiritual good of the people of God, rather than his own inclinations. He should, moreover, remember that the selection of different parts is to be made in agreement with those who have some role in the celebration, including the faithful, in regard to the parts that more directly pertain to each.*
>
> *Since, indeed, a variety of options is provided for the different parts of the Mass, it is necessary for the deacon, lectors, the psalmist, the cantor, the commentator, and the choir to be completely sure before the celebration about which texts for which each is responsible is to be used and that nothing be improvised. Harmonious planning and carrying out of the rites will be of great assistance in disposing the faithful to participate in the Eucharist. (352)*

It is worth working through the *Instruction* to see how it uses these criteria. The presider is reminded that the homily is to nurture Christian living and should take some account of the needs that the people themselves feel (65). Pastoral considerations ought to drive decisions when there is a choice of readings (360, 361). The same can be seen with the permission to celebrate with a congregation a Mass for Various Needs, Various Occasions, or votive

Mass on days when they are expressly forbidden: *If, however, required by some real need or pastoral advantage, according to the judgement of the rector of the church or the priest celebrant himself, a Mass corresponding to such a need or advantage may be used in a celebration with a congregation* (376). The criterion of pastoral effectiveness is paramount in the planning of the funeral Mass, for the family of the deceased but also for the mourners in attendance:

> *Pastors should, moreover, take into special account those who are present at a liturgical celebration or who hear the Gospel on the occasion of the funeral and who may be non-Catholics or Catholics who never or rarely participate in the Eucharist or who seem even to have lost the faith. For priests are ministers of Christ's Gospel for all.* (385)

As presider then, the principal celebrant has oversight of the whole celebration. His personal preferences are to be put aside for the sake of full and pastorally appropriate celebration by all the members of the assembly. His personality and training play a part in the development of his presiding skills. The criteria for the choices he directs are linked to pastoral considerations, the genres and forms within the rite, and appropriate consultation.

HIERARCHICAL CONSIDERATIONS

There are a number of points about the *sacerdos* and the *presbyter* that are best gathered together in terms of the hierarchical understanding of the church. The bishop is responsible for the celebration of the Eucharist in the diocese, and aside from him, there is no legitimate celebration. In light of this, the *presbyters* are seen as helpers to the bishop (92). Furthermore, a role in the Mass has been provided for the bishop even if he has assigned another to preside (92).

There are various instructions in the GIRM that signify the hierarchical office of the *sacerdos* (4). He is given a particular place on the sanctuary (295, 310) and distinctive vestments (337). He is reminded that these furnishings are about office rather than any personal honor when the GIRM states that the presider's chair should not resemble a throne, and only a chair for the deacon should be near it. As well, the presiding celebrant's chair should be placed to facilitate communication between priest and assembly (310). Both the rite for the exchange of peace (154, 239) and the reception of Communion (85, 86, 160, 162, 242–49) are attentive to the distinction between the priest and the other members of the assembly. Concelebration is encouraged as a sign of the office of priest: *For it is preferable that priests who are present at a Eucharistic Celebration, unless excused for a good reason, should as a rule exercise the office proper to their Order and hence take part as concelebrants, wearing the sacred vestments* (114). This exercise of office is understood as a sign of unity across all the levels and actions that embody the hierarchy (199). This is especially so when concelebration is with the diocesan bishop (203). It falls to the bishop to regulate concelebration (202), within the norms of the *General Instruction* (199–251). This fits the nature of particular churches within the one church.

Entitlement to the exercise of priestly office should not be allowed to compromise the integrity of the celebration. Consequently, priests who arrive after Mass has begun are not permitted to concelebrate (206). The *Instruction* mandates that when at the altar concelebrants should not interfere with the action of the rites, obscure the clear view of the faithful, or inconvenience the deacon in the performance of his ministry (215). Concelebrants do not have to be seated on the sanctuary when there are large numbers, nor should their placement disrupt the coherent unity of the assembly, itself an expression of the unity of the entire holy people (294). Their participation within the Eucharistic Prayers is closely described so as not to cut across the role of the presiding celebrant. This includes a provision that the presiding celebrant determines whether the concelebrants join with him in praying the doxology (236). The presiding celebrant should wear a chasuble, though concelebrants may wear only alb and stole (209).

THE DEACON

Increasingly the Roman Rite is paying attention to the role of deacons in worship. The third edition of the *General Instruction* reflects this correction in our liturgical sensibility and mentions the deacon more frequently in the various lists of ministers. In hierarchical terms, the place of the deacon is among the ordained: *After the priest, the deacon, in virtue of the sacred ordination he has received, holds first place among those who minister in the Eucharistic Celebration* (94). He has his own proper functions at Mass: proclaiming the gospel, preaching, announcing the intercessions, assisting the priest at the altar, distributing Communion, in particular under the species of wine, and giving directions (94, 171). When it comes to making choices and preparing the liturgy the deacon falls under the same criteria outlined above for the priest. The *Instruction* contains a separate section that describes how Mass is to be celebrated when a deacon is present (171–86).

His place in the hierarchical order is set out much the same as for other members of the rank of the ordained. The deacon is seated alongside the presiding celebrant in the sanctuary (310). It is in the sanctuary that he exercises his ministry (295). He is assigned vestments proper to the order (338). The question of whether he should exercise his ministry at a particular celebration does not belong to the presiding celebrant: *When he is present at the Eucharistic Celebration, a deacon should exercise his ministry, wearing sacred vestments* (171).

This last point may well appear quite contentious, but it reflects a consistent theology of hierarchy in the *Instruction*. The eucharistic celebration is the action of Christ and the people of God arrayed hierarchically (16). The order of deacons is an order within the hierarchy, and by right has a place in the liturgy. There is a serious problem for the church when one of its hierarchical orders is nonexistent or overly restricted or simply ignored. If in the Eucharist the church is made manifest, then what are the effects on our understanding of the church when one of its orders is habitually absent? We can gain an insight into these effects by examining common thinking about the proclamation of the gospel. Many priests and people think that this role belongs to the presiding celebrant, mainly because this is our constant practice. This has quite negative effects. It leads to a diminishment of our appreciation of hierarchy, with all emphasis visibly falling on those ordained *sacerdos*. The priest can be left with the illusion that this is his proper ministry, which he can share with a deacon at his discretion. As well, the presiding celebrant, who should fall under the word with the people, now both proclaims and preaches it. The *General Instruction* reflects some of this ambivalence toward the office of deacons in two ways. The section devoted to describing the Mass with a deacon comes after the description of Mass without one. As well, whereas the *Instruction* contains a developed theology of the *sacerdos,* there is little about the deacon. There is simply the acknowledgment that the order has been held in high honor since apostolic times, and that the deacon has his own proper functions (94). Ultimately, our liturgical theology and practice about the function of those in sacred orders at Mass is focused on the priest, the *sacerdos*. Consequently, our thinking is truncated, and the manifestation of the church arrayed hierarchically is restricted.

THE LAY FAITHFUL

The lay faithful constitute an integral layer in the hierarchical church. In the celebration they are made manifest as the church. They form the bulk of that Christian people described as a chosen race, royal priesthood, holy nation, and people set apart (91). These aspects should become clear in the Eucharist. More particularly the faithful themselves are considered in the *General Instruction* as follows:

> *For this people is the People of God, purchased by Christ's Blood, gathered together by the Lord, nourished by his word. It is a people called to bring to God the prayers of the entire human family, a people giving thanks in Christ for the mystery of salvation by offering his Sacrifice. Finally, it is a people made one by sharing in the Communion of Christ's Body and Blood. Though holy in its origin, this people nevertheless grows continually in holiness by its conscious, active, and fruitful participation in the mystery of the Eucharist. (5)*

In the eucharistic celebration, then, the church is said to be manifest as the church when the faithful are gathered by God, are nourished by the word, offer their prayers of thanksgiving, and partake of Communion. What sort of church is made present when full, conscious, and active participation in the eucharistic mystery is restricted?

The faithful are given an integral part in the celebration of the Mass. They are to allow themselves to be led by the presiding celebrant, to listen to the presidential prayers with attention (32), and to take up their proper parts in the dialogues (34), acclamations, and responses (35). They are to participate in the prayers and chants said or sung in common by the whole assembly (36, 37). Their singing is given great importance (39, 40), as is their posture and gesture (42), and their prayerful sacred silence (45). The liturgy of the word makes no sense whatsoever unless the faithful can hear it. How can God speak to the people in the word, as the *Instruction* teaches (55), if the rite is not enacted well, or if the faithful do not participate attentively? They are to make the intercessions (69). The very gifts of bread and wine, along with any offerings for the poor, are to come from the faithful (73). They are given an active part in the Eucharistic Prayer when they are instructed to respond in the dialogue, sing the chants, acclaim the mystery, listen with reverence and silence, and close the prayer with their Amen (78, 79). The culmination of the liturgy comes at their reception of Communion, normally from hosts consecrated at that Mass (85). The participation of the people should be marked by a distinctive spirit, befitting the holiness of the people of God. The GIRM seeks that the gathered assembly be marked by a deep religious sense, charity toward all present, the absence of division or individualism, unity (95, 96), and also the willingness to take up particular ministries or functions when necessary (97).

Within the level of the laity the *General Instruction* establishes certain ministries, central to authentic celebration of the renewed liturgy: *It is moreover appropriate, whenever possible, and especially on Sundays and holy days of obligation, that the celebration of this Mass take place with singing and with a suitable number of ministers. It may, however, also be celebrated without singing and with only one minister* (115). The appropriate ministers are at least an acolyte, a reader, and a cantor (116). Among the range of offices are the two instituted ministries of acolyte (98) and reader (99), which are restricted to men (CIC 230). When instituted ministers are absent, their functions can be taken up by other lay men or women (100, 101). The GIRM lists other lay liturgical functions: psalmist, cantor, choir, sacristan, commentator, those who take up the collection, greeters and ushers, master of ceremonies (100–106). Added to this are members of the lay faithful who take up roles on special occasions, or in specific rites, such as the minister who can give a brief introduction to the Mass of the day (50, 124). In a similar vein, if the priest needs assistance with the distribution of Holy Communion he can call upon extraordinary ministers. These ministers can be called from among duly instituted acolytes, laity previously commissioned for the role, or members of the congregation (162).

The *Instruction* also reinforces the integrity of lay ministries. It reminds that acolytes and readers have their own proper functions that they must perform (98, 99). These are ministries in their own right and are not simply exercised at the permission or whim of the ordained. There is an appropriate vestment attached to the office, commonly the alb (336, 339). Different parts of the same office can be shared if there is more than one minister present (109). The performance of a duty can involve either commissioning, in the case of instituted ministries, blessing, or a temporary deputation (107). Issues of qualification (101, 102) and suitability (107) are raised but not addressed in any systematic way. Ministers should be involved in the planning and preparation of the liturgy: *He [the priest] should, moreover, remember that the selection of different parts is to be made in agreement with those who have some role in the celebration, including the faithful, in regard to the parts that more directly pertain to each* (352). At the same time, the lay ministers need to be aware that they serve the active participation of the faithful in their worship, work under the presiding celebrant, prepare according to the rites and liturgical books, and are to be responsive to the pastoral situation (111). In this the GIRM offers the reminder that dictatorial behavior is not the preserve of the ordained.

These offices are not the equivalent of separate ranks or orders within the laity. With perhaps two exceptions, the distinctive aspects of their ministries relate to service to the liturgy, not personal dignity or honor or privilege. When the GIRM instructs that a reader may carry the Book of the Gospels in the entrance procession (120d) the focus is on reverence for the word of God and the acknowledgment of the diversity of ministry within the liturgy. Similarly acolytes sit within the sanctuary, not out of rank or honor, but so as to serve the priest better. They are to sit separately from the presiding celebrant and deacon to avoid any misunderstanding about their status: *Seats for other ministers are to be arranged so that they are clearly distinguishable from those for the clergy and so that the ministers are easily able to fulfil the function entrusted to them* (310, also 189). At the same time separate seating avoids any propensity the clergy may have to think of the presiding celebrant's chair as a throne (310). In light of the *General Instruction* it is clear that the ministries of lector and acolyte are not steps for ordination, nor rungs on a hierarchical ladder, but offices or services or duties of the lay Christian faithful within the liturgy.

It comes then as a disappointment that these two instituted ministries are not understood in terms of baptism but of gender. There can be no distinction from baptism between a Christian laywoman or layman (Gal 3:28). As well, the possibility of any justification for refusing these instituted ministries to women is removed since the *Instruction* allows that a woman may be commissioned to fulfill all the functions of the acolyte or reader (100, 101), save the purification of the chalice (192, 284b). As a result, few dioceses throughout the world have instituted readers, and many do not have instituted acolytes. Unfortunately, this means that one further aspect of the diversity of the body of Christ is diminished, and the church is made manifest as awkwardly unbalanced. There is a second way in which the instituted ministries can be confused with orders. There seems to be no provision for either a time limit to holding an instituted ministry, nor a corresponding requirement for continuing formation as an instituted ministry. Perhaps these points are behind the consideration in the *Instruction* that the bishop is responsible for norms in a diocese regarding the office of those who serve at the altar (107).

CONCLUSION

It is important to be aware of how the GIRM under-stands the church arrayed hierarchically in the celebration of the Eucharist. There are tensions and unresolved ques-tions at play in the discussion. One is the role of the dioce-san bishop and the differentiation of his office from others who are also ordained *sacerdos*. There are the two under-standings of the celebrating priest as acting in the person of Christ and as president of the assembly, the body of Christ. There is the place of the deacon, and the rights and obligations of the faithful. Yet within this the *Instruction* puts forward a compelling vision of participation and cele-bration in worship: as pastorally appropriate, true to the genre of the prayers, and well planned and executed. We are left to ponder if someone from outside walks into our Mass, whether they would be struck by the diverse modes of the presence of Christ and feel something of the mystery of the church and the wonder of salvation.

CHAPTER FIVE

THE EUCHARISTIC CELEBRATION

The celebration of the Mass, as the action of Christ and the People of God arrayed hierarchically, is the center of the whole Christian life for the Church both universal and local, as well as for each of the faithful individually. In it is found the high point both of the action by which God sanctifies the world in Christ and of the worship that the human race offers to the Father, adoring him through Christ, the Son of God, in the Holy Spirit. (16)

In our final chapter we take up the question of how the Mass, as reflected in the GIRM, is understood to remember, invoke, and respond to the trinitarian Godhead. This allows us to ask further about how our document understands the nature of the Eucharistic action itself and what it "celebrates." To begin we will examine how the *Instruction* sets out the trinitarian underpinning of the Mass.

IN THE NAME OF THE TRINITY

The Mass opens and closes with the sign of the cross and an invocation of the divine name, Father, Son, and Spirit (124, 167). The eucharistic celebration is immediately a celebration of the redemptive love of the three-person God. As we will see, the theological focus of the people of God is fixed most directly on Christ. Yet the *Instruction* also speaks of the activities and responses of God the Father and of the Holy Spirit. As with all reflection on the Trinity, the differentiation of roles is not always clear-cut. The mystery of divine love does not fit in so easily with attempts at categorization. We will begin by examining the way that the GIRM speaks of God and then move on to the place of Christ and the Holy Spirit.

PRAYER ADDRESSED TO GOD

In the Mass the community offers prayer to God. This is seen in the Eucharistic Prayer (2, 78) and the collect prayers: *In accordance with the ancient tradition of the Church, the collect prayer is usually addressed to God the Father, through Christ, in the Holy Spirit, and is concluded with a trinitarian ending...* (54). The quotation indicates the care that has been taken to avoid separating too strongly the different persons in the Godhead, while reflecting the different roles that are ascribed to them. God is the object of our worship as the source of salvation. This is expressed in the explanation of the element of thanksgiving in the Eucharistic Prayer: *the priest, in the name of the entire holy people, glorifies God the Father and gives thanks for the whole work of salvation or for some special aspect of it that corresponds to the day, festivity, or season* (79a). In a similar vein the prayers in the General Intercessions are also offered to God for the salvation of all (69).

Nor is God understood as remote from our eucharistic worship. The *Instruction* describes the silence that is part of the dynamic of the opening collect prayer as a time for the worshipers to realize that they are in God's presence, and to make petition (54). In the scriptural readings God is said to be speaking to and nourishing the people: *For in the readings, as explained by the homily, God speaks to his people, opening up to them the mystery of redemption and salvation, and offering them spiritual nourishment; and Christ himself is present in the midst of the faithful through his word* (55). At another level again, God is understood to be sanctifying the people, indeed all creation, in the celebration of the Eucharist. It is one of the reasons given why the Mass is at the center of Christian life: *In it is found the highpoint both of the action by which God sanctifies the world in Christ and of the worship that the human race offers to the Father, adoring him through Christ, the Son of God, in the Holy Spirit* (16). Again we can see the interconnection established among all the members of the Trinity. The sanctification of the people is related to the manifestation of God's presence in creation and throughout history, so that ultimately God may be all in all (79f).

Before moving on to the role ascribed to Christ in the Mass it is worth exploring what the *Instruction* and the Roman Missal itself imply when it is said that prayer is customarily addressed to God the Father (54). This section has been slightly modified from the second edition of the *Instruction,* mainly with the addition of a footnote that gives references back to early Christian tradition: Tertullian (ca. 160–225), Origen (ca. 185–254), and the Council of Hippo (393). These patristic examples speak of prayer directed to God, to the Father of Jesus Christ the High Priest, and to the Father respectively. This should not be taken as an argument that collect prayers and intercessions must be addressed to God using the appellation *Father.* The references concern liturgical prayer itself, in which prayer is customarily addressed to the first person of the Trinity. The three patristic sources given all predate the actual creation and introduction of Latin collect-style prayers into the Roman Mass. The overwhelming majority of our collect-style prayers, developed within this patristic framework, addresses the divinity as God or Lord with or without naming other attributes. Very rarely is God addressed as *Father* in ancient Latin collects or in the *Missale Romanum 2002.*[1] Exceptions are found in the Eucharistic Prayers, as well as in the fixed prayers such as the sign of the cross and the

Lord's Prayer. In the main, the Roman tradition is made up of prayers addressed to God or Lord.

THE PLACE OF CHRIST IN PRAYER

Christ is seen as at the center of eucharistic worship. Through Christ, God is said to sanctify the world, and in Christ the faithful are to offer their adoration and prayers (16). Each collect-style prayer and Eucharistic Prayer is made explicitly through Christ (54, 77, 89, 79h). The Mass is said to take its form and structure from Christ's own actions and commands (1), since after all it is the Lord's Supper (17). In particular this refers to the Last Supper as the central symbol for the celebration of the paschal mystery:

> At the Last Supper Christ instituted the Paschal Sacrifice and banquet, by which the Sacrifice of the Cross is continuously made present in the Church whenever the priest, representing Christ the Lord, carries out what the Lord himself did and handed over to his disciples to be done in his memory. (72)

The same paragraph goes on to describe the correspondence between the liturgy of the Eucharist in Mass and the words and actions of Christ. At the heart of every eucharistic celebration is the memorial of Christ's passion and resurrection (17).

We opened this section with the way the *Instruction* ensures we understand Christ at the core of all our prayers. This presence of Christ is developed in four modes. The GIRM teaches that Christ is present when Christians gather in his name (Matt 18:20), in the person of his minister, in his word, and under the eucharistic species (27). It is the name of Christ that makes our gathering Christian. It is his word, especially the Gospel, that is spoken to us (29, 62). It is his minister that leads our prayers, which are in fact made through him. Indeed the Mass is only complete in Holy Communion, that sacred union with Christ and one another through the common eating and drinking of his Body and Blood. Such union in Christ and one another is the end point of the Christian life and the foretaste of the reign of God in our midst.

The *Instruction* offers a number of titles and categories to understand the meaning of Christ and of our salvation in and through him. Not surprisingly in a document on worship, a good number of them are priestly and sacrificial in character. Christ is described as the High Priest (4), a reference to his role as the one who offers our prayers. This is closely associated with his title as Mediator, bringing the faithful into unity with God and one another so that God may be all in all (79f). There is something here of that vision of Paul, who feels the whole of creation groaning in anticipation of a newfound freedom in God (Rom 8:25). The interpretation of the paschal mystery as sacrifice allows for Christ to be seen as Victim, spotless (95) and acceptable to the Father for our salvation (2). This corresponds well to the image of Christ as Lamb, found in the hymn the Gloria (53), but is also evocative of the final chapters of the Book of Revelation, which portray the glorious new heaven and new earth (Rev 21–22). It is the Lamb who was slaughtered that has brought salvation, the memorial of which we celebrate in the Eucharist (Rev 5).

The discussion of the altar in chapter V of the *General Instruction* also offers a christological image. The altar is described as the altar of sacrifice (296). The *Instruction* offers, however, a broader reading of the altar as a symbol of Christ. In paragraph 298 it reads: *It is appropriate to have a fixed altar in every church, since it more clearly and permanently represents Christ Jesus, the Living Stone (1 Pet 2:4; cf Eph 2:20)*. Ultimately, it is not the altar that is most important, most "fixed" in the building, but the living Christ to whom the altar points. It is worth examining both scriptural quotations, including the verses that surround them. The First Letter of Peter reads: *Come to him, a living stone, though rejected by mortals yet chosen and precious in God's sight, and like living stones, let yourselves be built into a spiritual house, to be a holy priesthood, to offer spiritual sacrifices acceptable to God through Jesus Christ* (2:4–5). It is Christ, then, who is the living foundation for the priesthood of the church, for the acceptability of our worship, and for our ongoing conversion. The image is built not primarily around Jesus' sacrifice; rather, it is attentive to God's love for him, which raised him from death so that he could be a living stone. The section from the Letter to the Ephesians has a different resonance:

> *So then you are no longer strangers and aliens, but you are citizens with the saints and also members of the household of God, built upon the foundation of the apostles and prophets, with Christ Jesus himself as the cornerstone. In him the whole structure is joined together and grows into a holy temple in the Lord; in whom you also are built together spiritually into a dwelling place for God.* (2:19–22)

There is some liturgical sensibility present but the emphasis falls more onto Christ as the foundation upon which the whole church is built and brought to perfection, and which is the guarantee to the church of God's presence. The cornerstone implies the radical belonging of all members as part of God's household. By the inclusion of these two scriptural references, the *Instruction* calls us to understand the Christ symbolism of the altar more broadly than through the category of sacrifice. In doing so, it invites us to deepen our theology of sacrifice.

Christ is not only portrayed though liturgical imagery. He is also seen in light of the paschal mystery understood as his work of propitiation, satisfaction (2), and the payment of ransom (*purchased by Christ's Blood* 5). Propitiation and satisfaction are metaphors expressing the experience of being brought to peace with God, that agreement has been

THE EUCHARISTIC CELEBRATION

reached in Christ between God and sinful humanity, and that no further recompense is necessary. Behind "ransom" and "purchase" are theologies that attempt to express the experience of feeling freed from the burden of overwhelming captivity and slavery. The emphasis in the different images does not fall on what God requires by way of payment; rather, it gives expression to the freedom Christ has brought.[2]

The *Instruction* contains an oblique reference to Christ as shepherd of his flock (11). It is called upon in a discussion of the teaching value that the Mass has, an effect recognized by both the Council of Trent and the Second Vatican Council. The Second Vatican Council saw that the use of the vernacular was of great catechetical advantage. Trent, too, had recognized this, but, unable for a range of reasons to move away from Latin, encouraged pastors to give instructions on the mystery of the Mass. The underlying concern is that despite the valid celebration of the Mass there remained the danger that Christ's flock could go hungry (11). The current use of the vernacular goes beyond catechetical concerns alone, and takes up the question of a better comprehension of the mystery: *[enthusiasm for the vernacular] has led, under the leadership of the Bishops and the Apostolic See itself, to permission for all liturgical celebrations in which the people participate to be in the vernacular, for the sake of a better comprehension of the mystery being celebrated* (12).

Christ is not only pictured as at watch in the present. The *Instruction* alludes to his return at the fullness of time, setting this in the context of liturgical singing: *The Christian faithful who gather together as one to await the Lord's coming are instructed by the Apostle Paul to sing together psalms, hymns, and spiritual songs (cf Col 3:16)* (39). While this aspect of faith in Christ is not developed, it parallels an emphasis in the theology of the Mass as banquet.

Just as the *Instruction* admonishes that prayer is made to God the Father, it has to be acknowledged that in the Mass some prayers are made to Christ. The Lord Have

Mercy (52), Gloria (53), prayer for peace (154), Lamb of God (83), and even some collect-style prayers attest to this. It remains the rule, however, that in the eucharistic celebration prayer is addressed to God, through Christ, in the Spirit.

While the understanding of Christ is set within a trinitarian context, it can be said that in the GIRM there is too exclusive an emphasis on the place of Christ and a corresponding underplaying of the roles of the Father and the Spirit. This overemphasis reveals at least two problems. The first is the question of efficacy in Christian ritual. The sacramental theology that emerged from the great scholastic theologians of the Middle Ages was preoccupied with the question of causality: how something is brought about and why a particular celebration is efficacious. It was felt important to ensure that an action, especially a sacrament, was enacted efficaciously. The Reformation further highlighted this way of thinking about liturgy and ritual. The Protestant reformers attacked the veracity of the Mass as a sacrifice and the veracity of the Catholic theology of priesthood; in response, the Catholic Counter-Reformation stressed the sacrifice of the Mass. The integrity of the priesthood was a cornerstone in this defense, since a valid priesthood meant that the sacrament was efficacious. A consequence was that the Roman Church was able to justify the continuation of customs such as priests celebrating Mass with no one else receiving Communion, priests celebrating Mass with no one else present, and the system of Mass stipends. The *General Instruction* is also involved in this debate. The Eucharist is the action of Christ and the church. But do other members of the community besides the priest have to be present? A response in the GIRM is as follows:

> *Even if it is sometimes not possible to have the presence and active participation of the faithful, which bring out more plainly the ecclesial nature of the celebration, the Eucharistic Celebration always retains its efficacy and dignity because it is the action of Christ and the Church, in which the*

priest fulfils his own principal office and always acts for the people's salvation. (19)

Our concern here is the Christology in the *Instruction*. There is a danger of distortion when the emphasis falls too simply on the Eucharist as an action of Christ, seemingly outside of the workings of God and the Spirit. Similarly, there is also danger of distortion when the action of Christ and the action of the church are so closely connected without paying attention to the trinitarian context. This lack of context can allow for too quick an identification between any individual human and Christ, underplaying the gap between God and the human creature. It can also facilitate too quick a reduction of the body of Christ, the baptized, to a single representative, underplaying the interconnectedness of all the members of the body. The question of the efficacious nature of a celebration is important. It should not, however, be the primary dynamic for the exploration of the actions of Christ in our worship. Nor should it be discussed outside a liturgical theology of grace that insists that all our actions begin, are carried through, and are brought to their completion in God's love and only in God's love.

A second area of concern is the way the GIRM speaks of Christ as present in the word (29, 62). It is clearest in paragraph 29: *When the Sacred Scriptures are read in the Church, God himself speaks to his people, and Christ, present in his own word, proclaims the Gospel.* The identification of the Gospel reading with Christ has long liturgical pedigree, not in the least because it builds upon the appreciation of the Gospels as narratives shaped around the life and actions of Jesus. Yet contemporary scholarship on scripture leads us to ask whether such a simple identification is desirable. The liturgical preference for the Gospels does not do adequate justice to the inspired nature of the letters of Paul or other New Testament writings. As well, it makes it difficult for the faithful to appreciate the books of the Old Testament in their integrity. There is no doubting the importance of the teaching that Christ is present in the word. A new understanding of this presence, however, is needed to uphold the Spirit-inspired nature of all the scripture, not just the works of the four evangelists. It is to this role of the Spirit in the *Instruction*'s understanding of our worship that we now turn.

THE ROLE OF THE HOLY SPIRIT

Just as liturgical prayer is made to God, it is offered in the Holy Spirit. The *Institutio* sets this out in a number of places. It is applied to the opening collect prayer: *the collect prayer is usually to God the Father, through Christ, in the Holy Spirit* (54). Unfortunately, this is not the case with the other two collect-style prayers, the prayer over the gifts and the prayer after Communion, which remain described as prayers made in Christ (77, 89). The Eucharistic Prayer also is said to be offered in the Holy Spirit (78), with the epiclesis attributed to the power of the Spirit: *by means of particular invocations, the Church implores the power of the Holy Spirit that the gifts offered by human hands be consecrated* (79c). Both these references to the Spirit in the Eucharistic Prayer have been added in the third edition of the GIRM. There is a third action ascribed to the Spirit within the Eucharistic Prayer during the "offering": *in this very memorial, the Church— and in particular the Church here and now gathered—offers in the Holy Spirit the spotless Victim to the Father* (79f). The image, rich and complex, ultimately leads the faithful to understand that their worship is from God and taken up into God. The entire prayer is brought to a close with the doxology, a sung praise to the Father, made through Christ in unity with the Spirit (79h).

The Spirit is understood to be active in other ways during the liturgy. In its description of the Gloria, the *Instruction* writes of the role of the Spirit in gathering the church: *The "Gloria" is a very ancient and venerable hymn in which the Church, gathered together in the Holy Spirit, glo-*

rifies and entreats God the Father and the Lamb (53). A central role in the efficacy of the liturgy of the word is ascribed to the Spirit: *During the Liturgy of the Word, it is also appropriate to include brief periods of silence, accommodated to the gathered assembly, in which, at the prompting of the Holy Spirit, the word of God may be grasped by the heart and a response through prayer may be prepared* (56).

The Holy Spirit is also mentioned in the discussion, early in the *Instruction,* on the underlying unity across the breadth of the church's liturgical practices and traditions: *Moreover, this broader view allows us to see how the Holy Spirit endows the People of God with a marvellous fidelity in preserving the unalterable deposit of faith, even amid a very great variety of prayers and rites* (9). The same paragraph calls for profound study of the entire ancient liturgical tradition, Semitic, Greek, and Latin. There is a little irony here. This is the first reference to the Holy Spirit in the GIRM, yet it does not deal with prayer or the Eucharist, but with the "norm" of patristic tradition and the necessary guarantee of fidelity. One of the most normative aspects of early Christian thought about the Eucharist was the central role played by the Spirit. With its strong christological focus, the *Institutio* remains too reserved about the Spirit in our prayer.

THE EUCHARISTIC ACTION

What does the *General Instruction* say about the nature of the action that is the celebration of the Mass? No single answer or concept suffices. A range of terms and ideas are used, often interwoven, to bring out something of the meaning and significance of this liturgical act. They are attempts to give flesh to the twofold action of the Mass: God's action of sanctifying the world in Christ, and the worship of God by the human race, made through Christ and in the Spirit (16).

THE MEMORIAL OF CHRIST'S SACRIFICE

The *Instruction* opens with a reaffirmation of the sacrificial nature of the Mass. It is establishing an immediate connection with the teaching of the Council of Trent (2). By doing so, it attempts to assuage fears in the post–Vatican II church that the liturgical changes were too radical and threatened a change in doctrine. Yet the GIRM neither relies solely on this theology nor leaves it undeveloped. As well, the *Instruction* avoids the trap of differentiating too wildly between the Mass as a sacrifice and as a meal. Rather, its theological vision is more integrated and balanced.

We can best begin with a section from the second paragraph of our document. It seeks to set out a teaching that is in accord with our eucharistic tradition. The first and primary sacrifice, of which we should never lose sight, is the sacrifice of Christ on the cross. At the heart of the Mass is the paschal mystery, here understood through the lens of Jesus' death, all the while presuming his life, his resurrection, and his ascension, and the sending of the Spirit. The Mass is the sacrament of the cross. It is the memorial of the cross. The structure of this memorial, a meal, was instituted by Jesus. It was he who commanded that this form of a meal be the sacramental memorial of the paschal mystery celebrated by the church, his body. Because it is the memorial of the cross, the Mass sacramentally manifests what the paschal mystery brought to bear. It is, then, a sacrifice of the propitiation and satisfaction that Christ won. Because it is the act in which the church responds to the salvation that has come through Christ, it is the sacrifice of praise and thanksgiving of the people of God. Before drawing out these riches further, it is worth reading the paragraph itself:

> In this new Missal, then, the Church's rule of prayer ("lex orandi") corresponds to her perennial rule of belief ("lex credendi") by which namely we are taught that the Sacrifice of the Cross and its sacra-

mental renewal in the Mass, which Christ the Lord instituted at the Last Supper and commanded the Apostles to do in his memory, are one and the same, differing only in the manner of offering, and that consequently the Mass is at once a sacrifice of praise and thanksgiving, of propitiation and satisfaction. (2)

The *Instruction* goes to great lengths to keep these related concepts together. In paragraph 17 the Mass is understood as a meal. It is described as the Lord's Supper in light of its origins in the Last Supper. As well, this meal is the eucharistic sacrifice instituted by Christ and given to the church. The eucharistic sacrifice is seen as the memorial of both the passion and the resurrection. We find the same dynamic at work in paragraph 72, where the Mass is described unequivocally as sacrifice and meal. This is, as always, in the context of the paschal mystery, specifically the Last Supper and the cross. The meal is the sacrament that enables the sacrifice of the cross to be manifest in the present. As such it is the act of memorial that Christ himself commanded. The number reads:

At the Last Supper Christ instituted the Paschal Sacrifice and banquet, by which the Sacrifice of the Cross is continuously made present in the Church whenever the priest, representing Christ the Lord, carries out what the Lord himself did and handed over to his disciples to be done in his memory. (72)

It should be clear now that there is a complex set of images and teachings contained in these few sentences. We need, then, to explore the meaning of Christian sacrifice when applied to the Eucharist and the connection between sacrament and memorial, so that we can understand better the content of the GIRM.

SACRIFICE

Any discussion of how sacrifice is to be understood in light of the Mass has immediate difficulties to face. One is the range of meanings that are attached to the word, especially in anthropology and popular culture. Another is the range of Christian spiritual connotations that are evoked. A third, and one of the most intangible, is the variety of understandings that are brought to the surface when discussing the "sacrifice of the Mass," from careful theological statements to loose pious ramblings.

This is nothing new. Even in Jesus' time there were differing practices and understandings among the religions of the Roman Empire. Yet in Jewish thought there was a well-established tradition that understood that the one God had little use for burnt offerings and was more pleased with a response of love, including moral and just conduct: *For I desire steadfast love and not sacrifice, the knowledge of God rather than burnt offerings* (Hos 6:6, see also Hos 12:6). It is important for us to realize that the prophet Hosea refers not to a wrathful or vengeful God. Rather, his understanding of sacrifice is predicated on the love of God, a love that seeks only that the people repent: *I will heal their disloyalty: I will love them freely, for my anger has turned from them* (Hos 14:4).

From the first, Christians have understood that their salvation came about through the paschal mystery; the life, death, resurrection, and ascension of Jesus, and the sending of the Spirit. Within this, the death of Jesus was able to generate a theology of his sacrifice: in his death came our life. Every understanding of Christian sacrifice is built on this saving death. In the tradition of the prophet Hosea, this is comprehensively the act of a loving God. It is not an action for appeasing God. It is the very doing of God before we could even ask or pray or hope for relief from sin and death. In the utter incomprehensibility of God's love it made sense to see the death of Jesus as the saving sacrifice. Yet in using the term, Christians in the first centuries would have understood the complete irony in their choice of this word. By their nature sacrifices are repeatable. Christian sacrifice is the once-and-for-all sacrifice of Christ. In the polytheistic religions of the Roman Empire the offering of sacrifices included catching the attention of an absent, perhaps inattentive and possibly uncooperative God. Christian sacrifice came from God, was enacted by Christ, God incarnate, and was a demonstration of the total commitment in love that God has for creation and creatures. Sacrifice involved animals' blood and slaughter and a priestly class that profited from the meats left over. Christians had nothing to offer but their prayers and thanksgiving. They offered a sacrifice without altars, blood, death, or priests. They offered, and we offer still, a sacrifice of praise. The Christian Eucharist is a sacrifice unlike any other usage of the term.

SACRAMENT AND MEMORIAL

As a sacrifice, the Mass is interchangeably described in the GIRM as memorial or as sacrament. Catholic thought is more accustomed to the language of sacrament. The Eucharist is the sacrament of the cross. The sacrifice of the Mass is more properly and accurately the sacrament of the death of Christ at Calvary. The term *sacrament* arises from Latin theology, and the great theologians of the early western church. It is also a component of Greek Christian thought, though the theologians of the East preferred to use the term *mystery* rather than *sacrament.* Somewhat lost from sight has been the comparable biblical language of memorial. Jesus' command at the Last Supper to bless bread and cup and eat and drink in remembrance of him (Luke 22:19) is a profoundly sacramental ordinance. According to this Jewish form of speaking, in the memorial blessing and eating, the entire mystery of Jesus' death and resurrection is made present. Memorial does not mean reenactment, but the sacramental manifestation of the

111

paschal mystery. The *General Instruction,* attuned to the power of this scriptural language, has no hesitation in referring to the Mass as either memorial or sacrament.

THE SUPPER OF THE LORD

The form of the memorial sacrifice is a meal. This, too, is taken up in a range of images. Meal and blessing traditions are integral to the narratives of Jesus' death and resurrection. The Last Supper is the source of the command to celebrate the Eucharist: *At the Last Supper Christ instituted the Paschal Sacrifice and banquet* (72). The Mass then is carefully and properly understood as the Lord's Supper (17, 27, 319) in which the Lord's Body and Lord's Blood are eaten and drunk (72/3). The image of the Last Supper is an appropriate shorthand for the entire paschal mystery of Christ, just as above we saw how Jesus' death is used as a metaphor for his passion, death, and resurrection as a whole. As well, the Last Supper tradition in the scriptures ineluctably ties the meal to loving service through the recounting in John's Gospel of Jesus washing the feet of his disciples (John 13:1–20).

Supper points to food. At the eucharistic sacrifice we are meant to eat and drink. We are nourished at the table of the Lord with the Body and Blood of the Lord. Again we are reminded that this is Christ's supper. In the same moment we are to recall that this is an act of the absolute, unwavering, and undeserved love of God. The *Instruction* also describes the meal as Christ's banquet, a memorial of the paschal mystery, at which we feast on the spiritual food of the Body and Blood of Christ (80, 84, 304). The banquet image is evocative of the heavenly liturgy and the feast of the Lamb. More concretely it focuses the attention of the worshiping community on that bread and wine brought to the celebration, taken to the altar, blessed and consecrated, all with the intention of being our true food. If it is a banquet, then both the Lord's Body and Blood should be available for Communion (281). If it is a banquet, then Communion should be from the bread consecrated at that Mass, and only by exception from a store in a tabernacle (85). If it is a banquet, then the material for the eucharistic celebration should be recognizable as food (321), and perhaps even fresh (323). If it is a banquet, then we are called to feed others just as we are fed so graciously and gratuitously by God (73). If it is a banquet, we need to realize that the paucity of the fare, our bread and wine, works to rouse us to hunger for the fullness of life in Christ.

A related term for the celebration of the Eucharist is the "breaking of the bread" (83, 321). The expression is another from the vocabulary of the paschal mystery. This time the reference is to the resurrection, and Jesus' appearance to that pair of disciples fleeing down the road to Emmaus. The entire narrative has a strong eucharistic flavor, with the presence of Christ, the word burning their hearts, and the bread blessed, broken, and distributed (Luke 24:13–35). This event is summarized in the single term: *Then they told what had happened on the road, and how he had been made known to them in the breaking of the bread* (Luke 24:35). In the Acts of the Apostles, the breaking of the bread is synonymous with the celebration of the Eucharist (Acts 2:46).

Paul, too, uses the image of the single loaf to good effect. His emphasis, however, is that the unity of the body of Christ parallels the unity of the one loaf from which all are fed (1 Cor 10:16–17). Incongruously, it is the breaking of the unity of the loaf that brings about the unity of the body in love.

The *Instruction* collapses the perspectives of Luke and Paul, emphasizing the aspects of unity and charity:

> *The action of the fraction or breaking of bread, which gave its name to the Eucharist in apostolic times, will bring out more clearly the force and importance of the sign of unity of all in the one*

bread, and of the sign of charity by the fact that the one bread is distributed among the brothers and sisters. (321)

In effect, the *Instruction* offers three images for entry into the paschal mystery. The image of sacrifice relates us to the cross, the image of the Lord's Supper to the meal and foot washing in the upper room at the Last Supper, and the image of the breaking of the bread to the resurrection appearances of the Lord.

EUCHARIST AS CELEBRATION

Throughout the *Instruction* the Mass is described in terms of celebration. The opening paragraph contains a reference to Christ's celebration of the Last Supper. It immediately goes on to speak of the celebration of the Most Holy Eucharist and of the celebration of the Mass. The document constantly refers to the "eucharistic celebration." The Eucharist, as the action of Christ and his church, is first and foremost a celebration of thanksgiving because of our redemption in Christ. Celebration should not be reduced to enthusiasm, happiness, rejoicing, pleasure, fellowship, superficial or forced joy, going to a party. Its primary meaning is theological rather than emotional or social.

We celebrate that Christ has overcome all obstacles. Sin, evil, injustice, and violence no longer have the last word. Our worship is the celebration of this victory. We celebrate in faith, and rejoice in hope, that the life, death, and resurrection of Jesus, and his sending of the Spirit, are the absolute orientation of our lives. They are the source and guide of our love and compassion. They also ground our wonder. Grace abounds. In effect, our eucharistic worship has only one aim. We celebrate over and over—in season and out, in symbol, song, word, and gesture—that Christ is our hope and that the Spirit dwells with us. Every

Eucharist plunges us anew into that baptismal truth. The evidence of Jesus' own life, lived through the beatitudes he preached, reminds us that this is neither escapist, nor idealist, nor romanticist.

In authentic acts of thanksgiving we allow sin to be named and grief and evil to be lamented. As much as these may stretch our faith to the limit, even to name them is an act of hope grounded in Christ. Our celebrations are also marked by wonder; wonder that the Spirit has called such a group; that the word still speaks; that ordinary bread and wine are the defining symbols of the reign of God. It is little wonder that Jesus taught that where two or three of his followers were gathered in his name, there he was present (Matt 18:20). In all of this our eucharistic worship is not just the prayer of the converted but is an act in our ongoing conversion.

The *Instruction* understands the celebration of the Eucharist to be at the heart of all Christian life: *Furthermore, the other sacred actions and all the activities of the Christian life are bound up with it [the eucharistic celebration], flow from it, and are ordered to it* (16). It follows that because the nature of the eucharistic action is as a celebration, then by its nature it involves participation. The celebration encompasses God's ongoing sanctification of the world, the worship, and the adoration of the human race (16). According to the *Institutio* these are best accomplished as follows: *the entire celebration is planned in such a way that it leads to a conscious, active, and full participation of the faithful both in body and in mind, a participation burning with faith, hope and charity* (18). The act of thanksgiving involves participation in worship and ongoing sanctification and conversion. It encompasses our joy, our daily lives, and our lament for the tragedy that touches us and besets our world.

A SINGLE ACT OF WORSHIP

The eucharistic rite is a single act of worship, though made up of significant parts. This unity has more than one dimension. It betokens the unity of all the churches, a point that arises in the discussion on how many altars there should be in a church: *In building new churches, it is preferable to erect a single altar which in the gathering of the faithful will signify the one Christ and the one Eucharist of the Church* (303).

More particularly, the GIRM brings into focus the integrated nature of the liturgy of the Mass around the one "table." It is worth seeing the paragraph in full:

> *The Mass is made up, as it were, of two parts: the Liturgy of the Word and the Liturgy of the Eucharist. These, however, are so closely interconnected that they form but one single act of worship. For in the Mass the table both of God's word and of Christ's Body is prepared, from which the faithful may be instructed and refreshed. There are also certain rites that open and conclude the celebration.* (28)

Just as in the Emmaus story, the word and the blessing are inseparably linked. The paragraph offers a counter to views on the Mass that discount the liturgy of the word and prefer to concentrate only on parts of the Eucharistic Prayer, notably the consecration. The liturgy itself is a single table, providing instruction and nourishment. Its celebration requires the full, active, and conscious participation of all the assembly throughout the whole of the rite.

THE EUCHARIST AS THE RESERVED SACRAMENT

On rare occasions the GIRM refers to the reserved Sacrament of Christ's Body as the Most Holy Eucharist (315). This is understandable in a document as large and comprehensive as the *Instruction*. It also underscores that the Eucharist is an action, a celebration of praise and thanksgiving for salvation in and through the paschal mystery of Christ. The rarity and care with which the GIRM refers to the eucharistic species as the Eucharist should serve to remind us to be more careful in our own language about the reserved Sacrament. There is a danger that we can reduce the term to the reservation of the Sacrament of the Body of Christ, exclusive of the authentic and primary sense of Eucharist as the action of Christ and his body, the church.

CONCLUSION

The celebration of the Eucharist as the action of Christ and the people of God necessarily invites us to consider the trinitarian dimension of our worship and the nature of the action we are undertaking. Christian liturgical prayer is God centered, Spirit inspired, and Christ joined. While our focus falls on the role of Christ in prayer, the GIRM opens up the mystery of the threefold divine love.

Insofar as the Eucharist is an action in Christ, the *Instruction* puts before us the twofold action in the Mass of God's sanctification of the world in Christ and our response of Christ-borne, Spirit-infused worship. The theology of the GIRM focuses on Christ's paschal mystery and our sacramental celebration and memorial of the mystery of the Supper, the cross, and the resurrection. The interconnection of sacrifice, sacrament, meal, and memorial constantly reminds us of the richness of the mystery, the strengths of each particular focal point, and the need to keep all these in play in a single act of worship around the "table" of God's word and Christ's Body and Blood.

When we take up this trinitarian and paschal understanding of the eucharistic celebration we are forced to reassess both rigid rubricism and laissez-faire liturgical laxity. Neither suffices to properly celebrate our redemption. In all this the *Instruction* has attempted to take up the teaching in the Constitution on the Sacred Liturgy, where the memorial sacrifice is presented as: *a sacrament of love, a sign of unity, a bond of charity, a paschal banquet in which Christ is consumed, the mind is filled with grace, and a pledge of future glory is given to us* (SC 47).

NOTES

CHAPTER ONE

1. Pius X, *Motu proprio* on the restoration of sacred music *(Tra le sollecitudini),* November 22, 1903, introduction, in Kevin Seasoltz, ed., *The New Liturgy: A Documentation,* 1903–1965 (New York: Herder and Herder, 1966), 4.

2. See Pius XI, Apostolic Constitution *The Liturgy and the Gregorian Chant (Divini cultus),* December 20, 1928, in Seasoltz, *New Liturgy,* 58–63; and Pius XII, encyclical *The Sacred Liturgy (Mediator Dei),* November 20, 1947, in Seasoltz, *New Liturgy,* 107–59.

CHAPTER TWO

1. The tension between the universal church and the particular church is reflected within the congregations in the Vatican itself. See the response to then Cardinal Ratzinger by Cardinal Kasper, "On the Church—A Friendly Reply to Cardinal Ratzinger," *America* (April 23, 2001) and *The Furrow* 52 (2001): 323–32.

2. For an extended discussion of symbol, sacrament, and the life of faith, see Louis-Marie Chauvet, *Symbol and Sacrament: A Sacramental Reinterpretation of Christian Existence,* trans. Patrick Madigan and Madeleine Beaumont, A Pueblo Book (Collegeville, MN: Liturgical Press, 1995). The original was published in French in 1987.

3. Two important writings on this area are Paul de Clerck, "'Lex orandi, lex credendi': The Original Sense and Historical Avatars of an Equivocal Adage," *Studia Liturgica* 24 (1994): 174–200; and chapter 1 in Kevin Irwin, *Context and Text: Method in Liturgical Theology,* A Pueblo Book (Collegeville, MN: Liturgical Press, 1994).

CHAPTER THREE

1. See SC 21 where the term is used twice.

CHAPTER FOUR

1. See Gerard Moore, *Vatican II and the Collects for Ordinary Time: A Study in the Roman Missal (1975)* (Bethesda: Catholic Scholars Press, 1998), 28–34, 58–66.

2. Mark 14:22–25; Matt 26:26–29; Luke 22:15–20; 1 Cor 11:23–26.

3. *Guidelines for Admission to the Eucharist between the Chaldean Church and the Assyrian Church of the East,* July 20, 2001, published by the Pontifical Council for Promoting Christian Unity, in agreement with the Congregation for the Doctrine of the Faith and the Congregation for Oriental Worship.

4. See David N. Power, *The Sacrifice We Offer: The Tridentine Dogma and Its Reinterpretation* (New York: Crossroad, 1987), 74, 79.

CHAPTER FIVE

1. To confirm this I examined 1,770 collects, prayers over the gifts, post-Communion prayers, prayers over the people, and the collects within various rites such as those that close the readings for the Easter Vigil. Unavoidably some prayers were counted more than once if they were used for different Masses. Regardless of

this inconsistency, the results were overwhelming. Of 1,770 col-lect-style prayers examined, only eighteen used the appellation *Father (Pater)*. By contrast, 1,748 orations used *Deus, Dominus,* or *Domine Deus.* Three collects were found addressed to Jesus (December 24, Morning Mass, collect; September 14, Exalt Holy Cross, post-Communion; votive Mass 4, Myst Holy Cross, post-Communion). Interestingly a collect in the 1975 Missal addressed to Jesus has since been rewritten with an invocation of God, *Deus* (See MR1975, Common BMV 3, collect and the revision MR2002, Common BMV 7, collect). One prayer had no direct invocation (Masses for Various Necessities, 39, post-Communion). For a discussion of how God is named in the Latin collects for Ordinary time in the 1975 Missal, see Moore, *Vatican II and the Collects for Ordinary Time,* 621–27.

2.   For a helpful excursion into the New Testament theology of the experience of grace, see Edward Schillebeeckx, *Christ: The Experience of Jesus as Lord,* trans. John Bowden (New York: Seabury Press, 1980), 463–514.